Contents

Introduction

Russian in your pocket gives you the language you need to cover all the situations you are likely to meet on a holiday or short trip to the Soviet Union, from arriving in the country and dealing with Customs and hotel staff to finding your way around on public transport and making contact with ordinary Russian people.

In addition to simple phrases, some useful information has been included to provide practical help in each situation, while the Wordlist at the end is handy for reference. Each phrase is transliterated into the Latin alphabet, following as closely as possible the way in which it sounds. The Russian version is given directly beneath so that if difficulties arise, you can show the book to your waiter, taxi-driver, shop assistant and so on.

It is advisable to study the pronunciation section opposite and familiarise yourself with the Cyrillic script before you leave on your trip, and if you can master some of the basic expressions on pages 7–10, so much the better. The Russians you meet will be appreciative and you will find your efforts are well worthwhile.

Счастливого пути!

Pronunciation

- It is worth making the effort to master the Cyrillic alphabet so that you will be able to decipher some of the many signs, street names, metro stations and so on that you will encounter on your trip. The alphabet has 33 letters, many of which are the same in English.

The Russian alphabet

Letter	Sound	Example
А а	a	as in *c**a**t*
Б б	b	as in ***b**at*
В в	v	as in ***v**at*
Г г	g	as in ***g**ap*
Д д	d	as in ***d**og*
Е е	ye	as in ***ye**t*
Ё ё	yo	as in ***yo**ghurt*
Ж ж	su	as in *mea**su**re*
З з	z	as in ***z**oo*
И и	ee	as in *k**ee**p*
Й й	y	as in *to**y***
К к	k	as in ***k**ing*
Л л	l	as in *bott**le***
М м	m	as in ***m**at*
Н н	n	as in ***n**et*
О о	o	as in *f**o**r*
П п	p	as in ***p**et*
Р р	r	as in ***r**an*
С с	s	as in ***s**ap*
Т т	t	as in ***t**ree*
У у	oo	as in *sh**oo**t*
Ф ф	f	as in ***f**ill*
Х х		similar to *ch* in *lo**ch***
Ц ц	ts	as in *pi**ts***
Ч ч	ch	as in ***ch**op*
Ш ш	sh	as in ***sh**op*
Щ щ	shch	as in *fre**sh** **ch**eese*
Ъ ъ*		hard sign (see note)
Ы ы		similar to *i* in *f**i**t*
Ь ь*		soft sign (see note)
Э э	e	as in *b**e**d*
Ю ю	you	as in ***you**th*
Я я	ya	as in ***ya**rn*

- The hard sign (ъ) is not pronounced, but is sometimes found between a consonant and a vowel to indicate that these should be pronounced separately. The soft sign (ь) at the end of a word softens the preceding consonant, and produces a sound similar to a short *y* (as in ***y**ell*).
- Russian is a strongly stressed language, and in this book the syllable that carries the stress is printed in bold type. Vowels which are unstressed are pronounced differently to stressed vowels, particularly unstressed **о** which sounds more like an *a*, and unstressed **е** and **я** which are similar to *i*.
- Note that the Russian letter **г** (*g*) is pronounced like a *v* in many words ending in *-ого* and *-его*. Consonants at the end of words may also be pronounced slightly differently from the way in which they are written. The sound щ (transliterated as *shch*) is often run together in Russian speech and sounds more like *sh*.
- The system of transliteration used in this book is intended to follow English pronunciation as far as possible. Note, however, that the sound *ye* (Russian **е**), which appears at the end of many words, is pronounced as in ***y**et*; the sound *kh* (Russian **х**) is similar to *ch* in Scottish *lo**ch*** or German *Ba**ch***; and the sound *zh* (Russian **ж**) is like *su* in *mea**su**re*. The letters **ай**, transliterated *ay*, are pronounced *eye*; **ей** (*yei*) is pronounced *yay-ee*, and **ой** is transliterated and pronounced *oy*.
- Note that Russian adjectives, and verbs in the past tense, have different endings depending on whether the speaker is a man or a woman. Both versions are given where appropriate.

Basic expressions

For greetings, etc., see page 130.

yes — *da*
да

no — *nyet*
нет

please — *pa**zhal**asta*
пожалуйста

thank you (very much) — *spa**see**ba (bal**sho**ye)*
спасибо (большое)

You're welcome — *Pa**zhal**asta*
Пожалуйста

Excuse me — *Eezvee**neet**ye*
Извините

Sorry — *Veena**vat*** **(man)**/*Veena**va**ta* **(woman)**
Виноват/Виновата

It's not important — *Eta ni **vazh**na*
Это не важно

Language problems

I don't understand — *Ya ni panee**ma**yoo*
Я не понимаю

I understand — *Ya panee**ma**yoo*
Я понимаю

Do you understand me? — *Viy panee**ma**yetye min**ya**?*
Вы понимаете меня?

Do you speak English? — *Viy gava**reet**ye pa-an**glee**skee?*
Вы говорите по-английски?

I don't speak Russian — *Ya ni gavar**yoo** pa-**roo**skee*
Я не говорю по-русски

I only speak a little Russian — *Ya **tol**ka nim**nog**a gavar**yoo** pa-**roo**skee*
Я только немного говорю по-русски

Basic expressions

Does anyone here speak English?	***Kto**-ta zdyes gava**reet** pa-an**glees**kee?* Кто-то здесь говорит по-английски?
Please speak slowly	*Gava**reet**ye **myed**linyeye, pa**zhal**asta* Говорите медленее, пожалуйста
Please repeat it	*Pafta**reet**ye, pa**zhal**asta* Повторите, пожалуйста
Please write it down	*Zapee**sheet**ye, pa**zhal**asta* Запишите, пожалуйста
What does that mean?	*Shto **e**ta **zna**cheet?* Что это значит?
What is this called in Russian?	*Kak **e**ta naziy**va**yetsa pa-**roos**kee?* Как это называется по-русски?
I don't know	*Ya ni **zna**yoo* Я не знаю

Questions

What's that?	*Shto **e**ta?* Что это?
Who's that?	*Kto **e**ta?* Кто это?
Where is ...?	*Gdye ...?* Где ...?
When is ...?	*Kag**da** ...?* Когда ...?
How is ...?	*Kak ...?* Как ...?
Why is ...?	*Pache**moo** ...?* Почему ...?
Where to?	*Koo**da**?* Куда?
Where from?	*Atkoo**da**?* Откуда?

Which?	*K**a**koy*? **(masc.)**/*Ka**ka**ya*? **(fem.)** Какой?/Какая?
At what time?	*Fka**to**ram chas**oo**?* В котором часу?
How much is it?	***Skol**ka **stoy**eet?* Сколько стоит?

Requests

Have you got ...?	*Oo vas yist ...?* У вас есть ...?
Can I ...?	***Mozh**na ...?* Можно ...?
Could you help me?	*Viy ni ma**glee** biy mnye pa**moch**?* Вы не могли бы мне помочь?
Can you tell me?	***Mozh**itye ska**zat** mnye?* Можете сказать мне?
Do you know where ... is?	*Viy ni **zna**yetye gdye ...?* Вы не знаете где ...?
Please ...	*Pra**shoo** vas ...* Прошу вас ...
... give me	*... **da**eetye mnye* дайте мне
... bring us	*... preeni**seet**ye nam* принесите нам
... tell me	*... ska**zheet**ye mnye* скажите мне
... explain	*... abyas**neet**ye* объясните
... translate	*... pirivye**deet**ye* переведите
... show me in the book	*... paka**zheet**ye mnye **fkneeg**ye* покажите мне в книге

I like it	***E**ta mnye **nra**veetsa* Это мне нравится
I don't like it	***E**ta mnye ni **nra**veetsa* Это мне не нравится

Useful expressions

There is, there are ...	*Yist ...* Есть ...
Is there, are there ...?	*Yist lee ...?* Есть ли ...?
There isn't, there aren't ...	*Nyet ...* Нет ...
I'm ...	*Ya ...* Я ...
... hungry	*... ga**lod**yen* **(man)**/*ga**lod**na* **(woman)** голоден/голодна
... tired	*... oo**stal*** **(man)**/*oo**stal**a* **(woman)** устал/устала
I'm thirsty	*Mnye **khoch**itsa peet* Мне хочется пить
I have ...	*Oo min**ya** ...* У меня ...
I need ...	*Mnye **noozh**na ...* Мне нужно ...
Here is, here are ...	*Vot ...* Вот ...
Of course	*Kan**yesh**na* Конечно
Good!	*Khara**sho**!* Хорошо!

ARRIVAL AND DEPARTURE

- On arrival, you will need to go through passport control and customs, and to show your passport, visa and customs declaration. Make sure the customs declaration is returned to you, as you may have to show it when you leave.
- You are allowed to bring into the country personal effects, food for the journey and travel goods, but check customs regulations as to what you cannot bring in, e.g. Soviet currency, drugs, firearms, pornography and subversive literature. Currency, jewellery and other valuables must be registered on your customs declaration which you should retain for the return journey.
- When leaving the country, you are allowed to take out souvenirs and goods bought in Берёзка/ *Beriozka* (hard currency) shops, but you cannot take out Soviet currency (apart from one or two coins),

works of art and antiques such as icons, paintings, samovars, etc. acquired from other sources (without permission from the Ministry of Culture and payment of export duty).

Passport control

Here is ...	*Vot ...* Вот ...
... my passport	*... moy **pas**part* мой паспорт
... my visa	*... may**a** **vee**za* моя виза
... my luggage	*... moy ba**gazh*** мой багаж
I/We are ...	*Ya/Miy ...* Я/Мы ...
... from England/America/ Australia	*... eez **Ang**lee'ee/* *eez Amy**ere**ekee/* *eez Af**stra**lee'ee* из Англии/ из Америки/ из Австралии
... a tourist/tourists	*... too**reest**/too**reest**iy* турист/туристы
... a member/members of a group	*... chlyen/**chlyen**iy **groop**iy* член/члены группы
... here on business	*... zdyes pa dye**lam*** здесь по делам

You may see:

ПАСПОРТНЫЙ КОНТРОЛЬ ***pas**partniy kan**trol***	**passport control**

You may hear:

*Vash **paspart**, paz**hal**asta* Ваш паспорт, пожалуйста	**Your passport, please**
*Ka**ka**ya tsyel **vash**ei payez**d**kee?* Какая цель вашей поездки?	**What is the purpose of your visit?**

Customs

Here is …	*Vot …* Вот …
… my customs declaration	*… ma**ya** ta**mozh**ennaya diklar**at**seeya* моя таможенная декларация
… my suitcase	*… moy chema**dan*** мой чемодан
I have nothing to declare	*Oo min**ya** neeche**vo** nyet zaya**veet*** У меня ничего нет заявить
These are gifts/souvenirs	***E**to pa**dar**kee/souvi**neer**iy* Это подарки/сувениры
These are my personal belongings	***E**to may**ee leech**niye **vyesh**chee* Это мои личные вещи
I have bought/We have bought …	*Ya koo**peel*** **(man)***/koo**peel**a* **(woman)***/Miy koo**peel**ee …* Я купил (купила)/Мы купили
… cigarettes	*… seegar**yet**iy* сигареты
… cigars	*… see**gar**iy* сигары

... a bottle/two bottles	*... bootiylkoo/dvye bootiylkee* бутылку/две бутылки
... a watch/a camera	*... chasiy/fata-apparat* часы/фото-аппарат

I have already paid	*Ya oozhe ooplateel* **(man)**/ *ooplateela* **(woman)** Я уже уплатил/уплатила
Here is the receipt	*Vot kveetantsiya* Вот квитанция

You may see:

ТАМОЖНЯ *tamozhnya*	**customs**
ОСМОТР БАГАЖА *asmotr bagazha*	**luggage examination**

You may hear:

Eta vash bagazh? Это ваш багаж?	**Is that your luggage?**
Atkroitye chemadan Откройте чемодан	**Open your suitcase**
Daeetye vashoo diklaratseeyoo Дайте вашу деклара-цию	**Show me your declaration**
Zapolneetye etat tamozhenniy blank Заполните этот таможенный бланк	**Fill in this customs form**
Raspeesheetyes Распишитесь	**Sign here**
Viy dalzhniy ooplateet poshleenoo Вы должны уплатить пошлину	**You'll have to pay duty**

Currency exchange

- Money (деньги/***dyen**gee*) can be changed at airports, banks and hotel currency exchange desks on production of the currency declaration filled out at customs. Receipts should be kept in order to change it back when you leave.
- Travellers' cheques and foreign currency can be used in Intourist hotels and restaurants, and hard currency shops, so it is not generally necessary to change large amounts into roubles.
- Note that it is illegal to change money on the black market (where the rate may be up to ten times the official rate) and that you may be offered counterfeit notes.
- The Russian rouble is divided into 100 kopecks. Roubles come in notes of 1, 3, 5, 10, 25, 50 and 100, and there is a silver 1-rouble coin. Kopecks are silver or copper coins.

Where is the exchange office/bank?	*Gdye ab**myen**niy poonkt/bank?* Где обменный пункт/банк?
Where can I change ...?	*Gdye **mozh**na abmin**yat** ...?* Где можно обменять ...?
... money	*... **dyen**gee* деньги
... foreign currency	*... val**yoot**oo* валюту
... travellers' cheques	*... da**rozh**niye **chek**ee* дорожные чеки
... English pounds	*... an**glees**keeye **foon**tiy* английские фунты
... American dollars	*... amiree**kans**keeye **doll**ariy* американские доллары

I want to change ...	*Ya kha**choo** abmin**yat*** Я хочу обменять ...
... £20/£50	*... **dvat**sat **foon**taf/pitdis**yat** **foon**taf* двадцать фунтов/ пятьдесят фунтов
... $30/$100	*... **treed**sat **doll**araf/sto **doll**araf* тридцать долларов/сто долларов
Can you give me some small change?	*Viy **mozh**etye dat mnye **myel**ach?* Вы можете дать мне мелочь?
Can you change 100 roubles?	*Viy **mozh**etye razmin**yat** sto rooбl**yei**?* Вы можете разменять сто рублей?

You may see:

ОБМЕН ДЕНЕГ *Ab**myen** **dyen**ik*	**Currency exchange (office)**
ВАЛЮТНЫЙ КУРС *Val**yoot**niy koors*	**Rate of exchange**

You may hear:

***Da**eetye **vash**oo diklar**at**seeyoo, pa**zhal**asta* Дайте вашу декларацию, пожалуйста	**Give me your (customs) declaration, please**
*Vot vam kvee**tant**seeya* Вот вам квитанция	**Here's your receipt**
*Raspee**sheet**yes, pa**zhal**asta* Распишитесь, пожалуйста	**Sign here, please**

ACCOMMODATION

- Accommodation must be arranged before arriving in the Soviet Union, as visas are only issued when it has been confirmed. Intourist keeps a list of hotels, and although it is possible to make your own arrangements through them, rates are not cheap for foreigners who choose to travel independently. Hotels are extremely full between July and September, when single rooms may be in short supply.
- Joining an organised trip – whether tourist, educational or trade – is probably the best way of visiting the country. Tourist accommodation is generally first class, and consists of twin-bedded rooms with bath or shower, WC and telephone. It is not generally possible to guarantee what hotel you will be staying at until you actually arrive in the country.

- On arrival, you may have to fill in a registration form (регистрационный лист/*rigeestratseeo**n**niy leest*), and you will receive a hotel pass (пропуск/***propo**osk*) or card (карточка/***kart**achka*). In large hotels, you will not be allowed past the front door without first showing your pass.

Booking in at a hotel

We have booked ...	*Miy zakaz**alee** **nom**ir* Мы заказали номер
... a single room	*... adna**myest**niy **nom**ir* одноместный номер
... a double room	*... dvookh**myest**niy **nom**ir* двухместный номер
... a twin-bedded room	*... **nom**ir s dvoo**spal**noy **krov**atyoo* номер с двуспальной кроватью
... with bath/shower	*... s**van**noy/s**doosh**em* с ванной/с душем
... with private toilet	*... sa sva**eem** twal**yet**am* со своим туалетом
... with a balcony	*... sbal**kon**am* с балконом
My name is ...	*Mi**nya** za**voot** ...* Меня зовут ...
I am staying/We are staying for three days/a week	*Ya pra**bood**oo/Miy pra**bood**yem tree dnya/ ni**dyel**yoo* Я пробуду/Мы пробудем три дня/неделю
What's my room number?	*Ka**koy** **nom**ir?* Какой номер?

On what floor?	*Na ka**kom** eta**zhe**?* На каком этаже?
Please carry my luggage to the room	*Atnye**seet**ye moy ba**gazh** **fno**mir, pa**zhal**asta* Отнесите мой багаж в номер, пожалуйста
Give me the key to room no. 8	***Da**eetye klyooch at **no**mira **vos**yem* Дайте ключ от номера восемь
Where can I leave the car?	*Gdye **mozh**na pas**ta**veet ma**sheen**oo?* Где можно поставить машину?

What time ...?	*Fka**to**ram cha**soo** ...?* В котором часу ...?
... is breakfast/lunch/supper?	*... **zaf**trak/ab**yed**/oo**zh**een?* завтрак/обед/ужин?
... does the hotel shut at night?	*... zakriy**va**yetsa gas**teen**eetsa **noch**yoo?* закрывается гостиница ночью?

You may hear:

*Vash **pas**part, pa**zhal**asta* Ваш паспорт, пожалуйста	**Your passport, please**
*Za**pol**neetye rigeestratsee**on**niy leest* Заполните регистрационный лист	**Fill in a registration form**
*Raspee**sheet**yes, pa**zhal**asta* Распишитесь, пожалуйста	**Sign here, please**

*Vash **pro**poosk/**vash**oo **kart**achkoo, pa**zhal**asta* Ваш пропуск/вашу карточку, пожалуйста	**Your hotel pass/card, please**
*Vash **nom**ir ...* Ваш номер ...	**Your room is number ...**
*na **pyer**vam etazhe* на первом этаже	**on the first floor**
na ftarom etazhe на втором этаже	**on the second floor**
*na **tret**yem etazhe* на третьем этаже	**on the third floor**
*na chet**vyor**tam etazhe* на четвёртом этаже	**on the fourth floor**
*navir**khoo*** наверху	**upstairs**
*vnee**zoo*** внизу	**downstairs**
*pa karee**dor**oo* по коридору	**down the corridor**

You may see:

КОНТОРА *kan**tora***	**Office**
ЗВОНОК *zva**nok***	**Service bell**
АДМИНИСТРАТОР *admeenee**strat**ar*	**Manager**
РЕСТОРАН *rista**ran***	**Restaurant**
КИОСК *kee**osk***	**Kiosk**
ЛИФТ *leeft*	**lift**

Staying at a hotel

- In larger hotels, a *di**zhoor**naya* (дежурная) or hotel attendant is assigned to look after the keys on every floor and generally keep an eye on things. She will run little errands for you, such as fetching extra blankets, etc., and it is worth keeping on friendly terms with her.
- Although tipping is officially frowned on, it is customary to tip porters, hotel staff, waiters, taxi drivers, etc., around 10%.
- Large hotels have a wide range of facilities, including kiosks selling cards, souvenirs, newspapers, stamps and envelopes, a currency exchange office, a post office, hairdresser's and possibly a sauna, as well as restaurants, bars and snack bars where food and drink are paid for in foreign currency.
- The hotel service bureau is a very useful place, and there is usually someone on the staff who speaks English. They will arrange theatre and concert tickets, excursions and car-hire, call taxis and book tables in the more popular restaurants for you.
- Breakfast is almost always taken in the hotel. See page 36 of the **Eating Out** section for further details.

Where is ...?	*Gdye na**khod**eetsa ...?* Где находится ...?
... the lift	*... leeft* лифт
... the bar	*... bar* бар
... the buffet	*... boof**yet*** буфет
... the toilet	*... twal**yet*** туалет
... the dining room	*... sta**lo**vaya* столовая
... the cafe	*... ka**fay*** кафе

... the restaurant	... *rista**ran*** ресторан
... the service desk	... *byoo**ro** ap**sloozh**eevaneeya* бюро обслуживания
... the newspaper kiosk	... *gaz**yet**niy kee**osk*** газетный киоск
... the post office	... ***poch**ta* почта
... the hairdresser's	... *pareek**makh**irskaya* парикмахерская

Hotel services

Hotel staff

chamber maid	***gor**neechnaya* горничная
doorman	*shvei**tsar*** швейцар
floor attendant	*di**zhoor**naya* дежурная
manager	*admeenee**strat**ar* администратор
porter	*na**seel**shcheek* носильщик
telephonist	*tilifa**neest*** телефонист
waiter	*afeetsee**ant*** официант
waitress	*afeetsee**antk**a* официантка

Come in	*Vaee**deet**ye* Войдите
Can I have breakfast/lunch in the room?	***Mozh**na **zaf**trakat/ab**yed**at **fnom**irye?* Можно завтракать/ обедать в номере?
Can I leave this in the safe?	***Mozh**na as**tav**eet eta **fsei**fye?* Можно оставить это в сейфе?
Could you change the sheets, please?	*Peremye**neet**ye, pa**zhal**asta, pras**tiy**nee* Перемените, пожалуйста, простыни
Can I have these clothes …	*Nil**zya** lee … **etoo** ad**yezh**doo* Нельзя ли … эту одежду
… cleaned	*… at**dat** f**cheest**koo* отдать в чистку
… ironed	*… pa**glad**eet* погладить
… mended	*… pachee**neet*** починить
… washed	*… pastee**rat*** постирать
Please wake me at 7 o'clock in the morning	*Pra**shoo** vas, razboo**deet**ye min**ya** v syem chas**of** oot**ra*** Прошу вас, разбудите меня в семь часов утра
I am expecting a letter/ a message	*Ya zhdoo pees**mo**/za**pees**koo* Я жду письмо/записку
Has anyone phoned?	*Mnye **kto**-ta zva**neel**?* Мне кто-то звонил?
I would like to make a phone call to England/America	*Ya khat**yel** biy pazva**neet** f**Ang**leeyoo/fAm**yer**eekoo* Я хотел бы позвонить в Англию/в Америку

Please bring me ...	*Preeni**seet**ye pa**zhal**asta ...* Принесите пожалуйста ...
... an adaptor	... *adap**tair*** адаптер
... an ashtray	... ***pyep**ilneetsoo* пепельницу
... a blanket	... *ade**yala*** одеяло
... a bottle opener	... ***shto**par* штопор
... coathangers	... ***vyesh**alkee* вешалки
... a glass	... *sta**kan*** стакан
... a hot-water bottle	... ***gryel**koo* грелку
... some ice	... *lda* льда
... a needle and thread	... *ee**gol**koo **sneet**koy* иголку с ниткой
... (another) pillow	... *(yish**cho** ad**noo**)* *pa**doosh**koo* ещё одну подушку
... a pillowcase	... *nava**loch**koo* наволочку
... a plug	... ***prop**koo* пробку
... a sheet	... *pra**stiyn**yoo* простыню
... some soap	... ***miy**la* мыла
... some toilet paper	... *twal**yet**noy boo**ma**gee* туалетной бумаги
... a towel	... *pala**tyen**tse* полотенце

I want to order …	*Ya kha**choo** zaka**zat** …* Я хочу заказать …
… a car	*… ma**shee**noo* машину
… a taxi	*… tak**see*** такси
… to the airport	*… faera**port*** в аэропорт
… to the theatre	*… fti**yatr*** в театр
… for … o'clock	*… na … cha**sof*** на … часов
Can you organise …	***Mozh**na arga**nee**zavat …* Можно организовать …
… an excursion	*… pa**yezd**koo* поездку
… a visit	*… pasyesh**chen**eeye* посещение
… to the ballet/to the circus	*… fbal**yet**/ftseerk* в балет/в цирк
Give me …	***Da**eetye mnye …* Дайте мне …
… an air letter	*… aveea-pees**mo*** авиаписьмо
… envelopes	*… kan**vyer**tiy* конверты
… postcards	*… at**kriyt**kee* открытки
… stamps	*… **mar**kee* марки
… a newspaper	*… gaz**yet**oo* газету
… cigarettes	*… seegar**yet**iy* сигареты

Complaints and problems

The … doesn't work	*Oo min**ya** … ni ra**bot**ayet* У меня … не работает
… air conditioning	*… kandeetseean**yair*** кондиционер
… blind	*… **shtor**a* штора
… heating	*… ata**plyen**eeye* отопление
… (table) lamp	*… (na**stol**naya) **lam**pa* (настольная) лампа
… lock	*… za**mok*** замок
… radio	*… **ra**deeo-pree**yom**neek* радио́-приёмник
… shower	*… doosh* душ
… tap	*… kran* кран
… telephone	*… tili**fon*** телефон
… television	*… tili**vee**zar* телевизор
… toilet	*… twal**yet*** туалет

I need an electric plug	*Mnye **noozh**na **shtyep**silnaya **veel**ka* Мне нужна штепсельная вилка
There's no hot water	*Nyet gar**ya**chei va**diy*** Нет горячей воды
The sink is blocked	***Rak**aveena za**sor**yena* Раковина засорена
There's no light	*Ni **gor**eet svyet* Не горит свет

The light-bulb's gone	*Pirigar**yel**a **lam**pachka* Перегорела лампочка
The window doesn't open	*Ni atkriy**va**yetsa ak**no*** Не открывается окно
The room's too ...	***Fnom**irye **sleesh**kam ...* В номере слишком ...
... cold	*... **khol**adna* холодно
... hot	*... **zhark**a* жарко
... noisy	*... **shoom**na* шумно
I don't like the room	***Nom**ir mnye ni **nra**veetsa* Номер мне не нравится
Have you got a larger one?	*Oo vas yist **nom**ir pa**bol**she?* У вас есть номер побольше?
... with a view of the sea	*... **swee**dam na **mor**ye* с видом на море
The room's dirty	*F **nom**irye **grya**zna* В номере грязно
I've forgotten my key	*Ya za**biy**l* **(man)**/*za**biy**la* **(woman)** *klyooch* Я забыл/забыла ключ
I have lost my key	*Ya patir**yal*** **(man)**/*patir**yal**a* **(woman)** *klyooch* Я потерял/потеряла ключ
I've lost my bag	*Ya patir**yal*** **(man)**/*patir**yal**a* **(woman)** ***soom**koo* Я потерял/потеряла сумку
I think someone's stolen my passport	***Doo**mayoo, shto oo min**ya** oo**kra**lee **pas**part* Думаю, что у меня украли паспорт
I don't feel very well	*Ya **plo**kha sib**ya** **choost**vooyoo* Я плохо себя чувствую

Call a doctor — *Viyzaveetye vracha*
Вызовите врача

Extra vocabulary

armchair	*krislo* кресло
bed	*kravat* кровать
chair	*stool* стул
door	*dvyer* дверь
guest	*gost* гость
hall	*vyesteebyool* вестибюль
iron	*ootyook* утюг
office	*kantora* контора
radiator	*radeeatar* радиатор
reception	*preeyom* приём
service bell	*zvanok* звонок
stairs	*lestneetsa* лестница
suite	*nomir lyooks* номер люкс
tariff	*tareef* тариф
voltage	*napryazheneeye* напряжение

Checking out

I am leaving/We are leaving ...	*Ya ooye**zha**yoo/Miy ooye**zha**yem ...* Я уезжаю/Мы уезжаем ...
... today/tomorrow/early in the morning	*... si**vod**nya/**zaf**tra/**ra**na **oot**ram* сегодня/завтра/рано утром
What time do I have to leave the room?	*F ka**to**ram cha**soo** **na**da asvaba**deet** **nom**ir?* В котором часу надо освободить номер?
We are in a hurry	*Miy **och**in spi**sheem*** Мы очень спешим
Please call a taxi	***Viy**zaveetye, pa**zhal**asta, tak**see*** Вызовите, пожалуйста, такси
Where can I leave my luggage?	*Gdye **mozh**na asta**veet** moy ba**gazh**?* Где можно оставить мой багаж?
Can I leave my case in the left luggage room?	***Mozh**na **asta**veet chema**dan** f **ka**mirye khran**yen**eeya ba**ga**zha?* Можно оставить чемодан в камере хранения багажа?
Take the luggage ...	*Atni**seet**ye ba**gazh** ...* Отнесите багаж ...
... downstairs	*... fneez* вниз
... to the taxi	*... ftak**see*** в такси
... to the left-luggage room	*... **fkam**yeroo khran**yen**eeya* в камеру хранения

Camping

- Camping for motorists is permitted at official sites only, and the itinerary must be arranged and agreed in advance – you can't just turn up! Payment is in Intourist vouchers.
- Some camp-sites (кемпинги/***kem**peengee*) are only open for three months in the summer, and by Continental standards, camping is fairly primitive.
- It is advisable to take all essential items with you. If you don't have your own tent, you can hire a tent or a hut. You can also hire camp beds, bedding and cooking equipment. Sites have washing facilities and showers, and may include a restaurant, post office and shops. There is generally a petrol station in the vicinity.

How far is it to the camp site?	***Skol**ka **yek**hat do **kem**peenga?* Сколько ехать до кемпинга?
Where can I pitch my tent?	*Gdye **mozh**na pa**sta**veet pa**lat**koo?* Где можно поставить палатку?
Can I park my caravan here?	***Mozh**na pa**sta**veet dom-aftafoor**gon** zdyes?* Можно поставить дом-автофургон здесь?
Here is my camping permit	*Vot moy **prop**oosk f**kem**peeng* Вот мой пропуск в кемпинг
Can I light a fire?	***Mozh**na raz-**zhech** kast**yor**?* Можно разжечь костёр?
Can I hire …	***Mozh**na vzyat na**prok**at …* Можно взять напрокат …
… a camp bed	*… pa**khod**nooyoo kra**vat*** походную кровать

... camping equipment	*... aba**rood**avaneeye **kem**peenga* оборудование кемпинга
... cooking utensils	*... koo**khon**nooyoo pa**sood**oo* кухонную посуду
... a frying pan	*... kas**tryool**yoo* кастрюлю
... a hut	*... **dom**eek* домик
... a sleeping bag	*... **spal**niy me**shok*** спальный мешок
... a tent	*... pa**lat**koo* палатку

Where is ...?	*Gdye na**khod**eetsa ...?* Где находится ...?

... the camp office	*... admeenees**trat**seeya* администрация
... the electric point	*... raz**yet**ka* розетка
... the iron	*... oot**yook*** утюг
... the restaurant	*... rista**ran*** ресторан
... the rubbish bin	*... **moo**sarniy **yash**cheek* мусорный ящик
... the shop	*... maga**zeen*** магазин
... the sanitary block	*... sanee**tar**niy blok* санитарный блок
... the tap	*... kran* кран
... the toilet	*... twal**yet*** туалет
... the washbasin	*... oomiy**val**neek* умывальник

Where can I buy ...?	*Gdye **mozh**na koo**peet** ...?* Где можно купить ...?
... a corkscrew	*... **shtop**ar* штопор
... camping gas	*... boo**tan**aviy gaz* бутановый газ
... food	*... pra**dook**tiy* продукты
... insect repellant	*... **sred**stva at nasi**kom**ava* средство от насекомого
... matches	*... **speech**kee* спички
... tent pegs	*... pa**lat**achniye pree**kol**iyshee* палаточные приколыши
... a tin opener	*... kans**yerv**niy nozh* консервный нож
... toilet paper	*... twal**yet**nooyoo boo**ma**goo* туалетную бумагу
... washing powder	*... stee**ral**niy para**shok*** стиральный порошок
How many vouchers do we owe you?	***Skol**ka ta**lon**af miy vam dalzh**niy**?* Сколько талонов мы вам должны?

You may see:

ПОСТАНОВКА ПАЛАТОК *Pasta**nof**ka pa**lat**ak*	**Pitching of tents**
ПИТЬЕВАЯ ВОДА *Peetye**vay**a va**da***	**Drinking water**
ВОДА НЕ ДЛЯ ПИТЬЯ *Va**da** ne dlya peet**ya***	**Non-drinking water**

EATING OUT

- State-run snackbars (закусочная/*za**koo**sachnaya*) and cafeterias (столовая/*sta**lo**vaya*) are often extremely crowded and rather uninviting places, and there are few Western-style cafes. Many snackbars are self-service, and in some there is no seating. A price displayed opposite a dish indicates that it is available (sometimes food has to be paid for in advance and the receipt handed to the waiter). Generally speaking, there are no set meals.
- Some eating places specialise in certain dishes: pies are eaten at a пирожковая/*peerazh**ko**vaya*, pancakes at a блинная/***bleen**aya*, dumplings at a пельменная/*pil**myen**aya* and shashliks at a шашлычная/*shash**liych**naya*. The кафе-кондитерская (*kafe-kandit**yer**skaya*) sells cakes and coffee, and ice cream parlours (кафе-мороженое/*kaf**ay**-ma**rozh**enoye*) are very popular. There are

many different varieties of ice cream available in the Soviet Union. A пивной бар (*peev**noy** bar*) is a beer hall. Pies, pastries and coffee can be bought at street snack stands, and vending machines dispense mineral water and cola. Beer and *kvass* (квас), a drink made from fermented bread, can be bought from street stalls. In hotels, theatres, etc., the buffet (буфет/*boof**yet***) also serves snacks.

- Lunch, served from 11 am to 3 pm, is the main meal, and always includes a soup course. The evening meal is served between 7 and 10.30 pm – restaurants tend to close early. Intourist hotel vouchers can be used to pay for meals in other hotels, but this should be arranged in advance. In bars reserved for foreigners, drinks must be paid for in hard currency. They often stay open until 2 am.
- A cafe (кафе) is the equivalent of a restaurant, and a restaurant (ресторан/*rista**ran***) is a place to go for a special evening out. It usually has a band and a dance floor. There are some good restaurants, notably those specialising in regional cuisine, but they are expensive and very popular, and should be booked ahead from the hotel service desk. The privately-run cooperative restaurants (ресторан кооператив/*rista**ran** kooperat**eev***) serve good food, but it is not cheap.
- When eating in a restaurant, coats and bags should be left in the cloakroom. The bill always includes service and, although tipping is not officially recognised, a tip of around 10% is generally appreciated.

I'd like something to eat	*Ya khat**yel*** (**man**)/*khat**yel**a* (**woman**) *biy shto-neeboot pa**koo**shat* Я хотел/хотела бы что-нибудь покушать
I'd like something to drink	*Ya khat**yel*** (**man**)/*khat**yel**a* (**woman**) *biy shto-neeboot **vi**ypeet* Я хотел/хотела бы что-нибудь выпить

Finding somewhere to eat

Where can I ...?	*Gdye zdyes **mozh**na ...?* Где здесь можно ...?
... get a snack	*... **biy**stra pirikoo**seet*** быстро перекусить
... have a coffee	*... **viy**peet **kof**ye* выпить кофе
... get a cheap meal	*... ni**dor**aga pa-ab**yed**at* недорого пообедать
Can you recommend a good restaurant?	*Viy **mozh**itye parikam**yen**davat khar**osh**ee rista**ran**?* Вы можете порекомендовать хороший ресторан?
I would like to reserve a table ...	*Ya khat**yel** biy zaka**zat** **stol**eek ...* Я хотел бы заказать столик ...
... for two/three/four	*... na dva**eekh**/tra**eekh**/chetvi**riykh*** на двоих/троих/четверых
... by the window	*... oo ak**na*** у окна
... in the corner	*... foo**gloo*** в углу
... for 7 o'clock	*... na syem cha**sof*** на семь часов
... for tomorrow	*... na **zaf**tra* на завтра
Is this table free?	***E**tat **stol**eek sva**bod**yen?* Этот столик свободен?

You may hear:

*Ya vas **sloo**shayoo* Я вас слушаю	**Yes? (What would you like?)**
*Ya rikamen**doo**yoo ...* Я рекомендую ...	**I recommend ...**
*K sazhal**yene**eyoo, etava oo nas si**vod**nya nyet* К сожалению у нас этого сегодня нет	**I'm sorry, it's off today**
*Viy **boo**ditye zaka**zi**yvat?* Вы будете заказывать?	**Are you ready to order?**
*Shto yish**cho**?/**E**ta vsyo?* Что ещё?/Это всё?	**Anything else?/Is that all?**
*Shto viy **boo**ditye peet?* Что вы будете пить?	**What would you like to drink?**

You may see:

СТОЛ ЗАКАЗАН *Stol za**ka**zan*	**Table reserved**
Дежурное блюдо *Di**zhoor**noye **blyoo**da*	**Dish of the day**
Фирменные блюда ***Fir**myeniye **blyoo**da*	**Specialities**

Breakfast

- Breakfast is often fairly substantial in the Soviet Union, with fruit juice, cold meats, cheese or sausage as well as rolls and jam. Cooked dishes include eggs, omelettes and pancakes with sour cream, a very popular accompaniment to Russian food. You will be offered a choice of tea or coffee. Tea is usually served in glasses without milk, though there may be a slice of lemon. In Russian households it is sometimes accompanied by jam.

Dairy products are very popular, and *kefir* (a yoghurt-type drink) is often served for breakfast.

Please give me ...	***Da****eetye pa****zhal****asta ...* Дайте пожалуйста ...
... pancakes	*... **bleen**cheekee* блинчики
... porridge (buckwheat)	*... **kash**oo* кашу
... rolls and jam	*... **bool**achkee svar**yen**yem* булочки с вареньем
... sausages (frankfurter type)	*... sa**sees**kee* сосиски
Do you have ...?	*Oo vas yist ...?* У вас есть ...?
... eggs	*... **ya**itsa* яйца
... boiled eggs	*... var**yon**iye **ya**itsa* варёные яйца
... hard boiled eggs	*... **ya**itsa **fkroot**ooyoo* яйца вкрутую
... soft boiled eggs	*... **ya**itsa **fsmyat**kooyoo* яйца всмяткую
... fried eggs	*... ya**eech**neetsa-gla**zoon**ya* яичница-глазунья
... ham and eggs	*... **ya**itsa svitchee**noy*** яйца с ветчиной
... an omelette (ham/cheese)	*... am**lyet** (s **siy**ram/ svitchee**noy**)* омлет (с сыром/с ветчиной)
Waitress, more/another ... please	***Dye****vooshka, yish****cho**** ... pa****zhal****asta* Девушка, ещё ... пожалуй-ста

Ordering snacks

I'd like ...	*Ya khat***yel** *biy* (**man**)/*Ya khat***yel***a biy* (**woman**) ... Я хотел бы/Я хотела бы ...
... coffee	... ***kof****ye* кофе
... two coffees	... *dva* ***kof****ye* два кофе
... tea	... *chay* чай
... with milk	... *smala****kom*** с молоком
... without milk	... *byez mala****ka*** без молока
... with lemon	... *slee****mon****am* с лимоном
... with sugar	... *s* ***sakh****aram* с сахаром
... without sugar	... *byez* ***sakh****ara* без сахара
... a cola	... *pepsi-****kol****oo* пепси-колу
... a fizzy orange	... ***fan****ta* фанта
... a fruit juice	... *frook****tov****iy sok* фруктовый сок
... an orange juice	... *apil****seen****aviy sok* апельсиновый сок
... an apple juice	... ***yab****lachniy sok* яблочный сок
... a tomato juice	... *ta****mat****niy sok* томатный сок
... a mineral water	... *meeni****ral****nooyoo va****doo*** минеральную воду
... lemonade	... *leema****nat*** лимонад

Eating out

I'll have ...	*Ya vaz**moo** ...* Я возьму ...
... a pie	*... peera**zhok*** пирожок
... a frankfurter	*... sa**sees**koo* сосиску
... an omelette	*... aml**yet*** омлет
... a pastry	*... pee**rozh**noye* пирожное
... a pancake	*... **bleen**cheek* блинчик
... an ice cream	*... ma**rozh**enoye* мороженое
Have you any sandwiches?	*Oo vas yist booter**brod**iy?* У вас есть бутерброды?
Give me a ... sandwich	***Da**eetye mnye booter**brot** ...* Дайте мне бутерброд ...
... cheese	*... s **siy**ram* с сыром
... ham	*... svitchee**noy*** с ветчиной
... salami	*... skalba**soy*** с колбасой
... caviar	*... seek**roy*** с икрой

Ordering a meal

Please bring me the menu	***Da**eetye, pa**zha**lasta, min**yoo*** Дайте, пожалуйста, меню
What do you recommend?	*Shto viy parikamen**doo**itye?* Что вы порекомендуете?

Please bring me ...	*Preeni**seet**ye, pa**zhal**asta ...* Принесите, пожалуйста ...
... an ashtray	*... **pyep**ilneetsoo* пепельницу
... a fork	*... **veel**koo* вилку
... a glass of water	*... sta**kan** va**diy*** стакан воды
... a knife	*... nozh* нож
... a napkin	*... salf**yet**koo* салфетку
... a plate	*... tar**yel**koo* тарелку
... a spoon	*... **lozh**koo* ложку
... a wineglass	*... **ryoom**koo* рюмку
... the mustard	*... gar**cheet**soo* горчицу
... the pepper	*... **pye**rits* перец
... the salt	*... sol* соль

Please give me some more ...	***Boot**tye **dob**riy, **da**eetye yish**cho** ...* Будьте добры, дайте ещё ...
... bread	*... **xhlyeb**a* хлеба
... butter	*... **mas**la* масла
... water	*... va**diy*** воды

Eating out

Bring another place setting/ chair	*Preeni**seet**ye yish**cho** a**deen** pree**bor**/stool* Принесите ещё один прибор/стул
I am a vegetarian	*Ya vigitaree**an**ets* (**man**), *vigitaree**an**ka* (**woman**) Я вегетарианец, вегетарианка
I don't eat meat/fish/eggs	*Ya ni yem **mya**sa/**riy**boo/**ya**itsa* Я не ем мясо/рыбу/яйца
What kind of meat is it?	*Shto **e**ta za **mya**sa?* Что это за мясо?

I'd like ...	*Ya xhat**yel** biy* (**man**)/ *xhat**yel**a biy* (**woman**) ... Я хотел бы/хотела бы ...

... a small portion	*... **mal**inkooyoo **port**siyoo* маленькую порцию
... a half portion	*... pol-**port**see'ee* пол-порции

Waiter/waitress!	*Afeetsee**ant**/**dye**vooskha!* Официант/девушка!
I'm/We're in a hurry	*Ya spi**shoo**/Miy spi**sheem*** Я спешу/Мы спешим
We've chosen/haven't chosen yet	*Miy **viy**bralee/Miy yish**cho** ni **viy**bralee* Мы выбрали/Мы ещё не выбрали
Thank you, I've had enough	*Spa**see**ba, das**tat**achna* Спасибо, достаточно

You may hear:

*Shto viy **boo**ditye ...?* Уто вы будете ...?	**What would you like ...?**
*... eez za**koo**sak* из закусок	**... for starters**

... *na **pyer**voye/fta**ro**ye* на первое/второе	**... for the first/second course**
... *na dis**yert*** на десерт	**... for dessert**
*Nyet, **nye**too* Нет, нету	**No, we haven't any**
*Kak vam **nra**veetsa ...?* Как вам нравится ...?	**How do you like ...?**
*Pree**yat**nava appi**tee**ta!* Приятного аппетита!	**Bon appétit!**

Describing food

It's very/too ...	***E**ta **o**chin/**sleesh**kam ...* Это оуень/слишком ...
... cold	... *as**tiy**la* остыло
... hot (spiced)	... ***os**tra* остро
... overcooked	... *piri**zhar**yena* пережарено
... raw	... ***siy**roye* сырое
... stale	... *nis**vezhe**ye* несвежее
... salty	... *sal**yon**oye* солёное
... tough	... ***zhyost**koye* жёсткое
... tasty	... ***fkoos**na* вкусно
... underdone	... *nido**zhar**yena* недожарено

Understanding the menu

● See also **Shopping for food** on page 101.

Закуски/*Zakuski* Starters

салат *salat*	**salad**
из огурцов *eez agoortsof*	**cucumber**
из помидоров *eez pameedoraf*	**tomato**
из крабов *eez krabaf*	**crab**
маслины *masleeniy*	**black olives**
ассорти мясное *assortee myasnoye*	**assorted cold meat**
ассорти рыбное *assortee riybnoye*	**assorted fish**
селёдка *silyotka*	**herring**
сёмга с лимоном *syomga sleemonam*	**smoked salmon with lemon**
заливная осетрина *zaleevnaya asyetreena*	**sturgeon in aspic**
чёрная/красная/паюсная икра *chornaya/krasnaya/payoosnaya eekra*	**black/red/pressed caviar**
креветки *krivetkee*	**shrimps**
винегрет *veenegret*	**Russian salad**
яйцо под майонезом *Yaitso pod mayonezam*	**egg mayonnaise**
маринованные грибы *mareenovanniye greebiy*	**pickled mushrooms**

Супы/*Soopiy* Soups

борщ *borshch*	**borstch (beetroot soup)**
щи *shchee*	**cabbage soup**
уха *ookha*	**fish and potato soup**
бульон с фрикадельками *boolyon sfreekadyelkamee*	**consomme with meatballs**

куриный бульон *koo**ree**niy bool**yon***	**chicken soup**	гороховый суп *ga**rokh**aviy soop*	**pea soup**
мясная/ рыбная солянка ***myas**naya/ **riyb**naya sal**yan**ka*	**spicy fish/ meat soup**	рассольник *ra**ssol**neek*	**kidney and vegetable soup**
		суп с лапшой *soop **slap**shoy*	**noodle soup**

Рыбные блюда/*Riybniye blyooda*
Fish dishes

карп *karp*	**carp**	камбала ***kam**bala*	**plaice**
треска *tris**ka***	**cod**	лососина *lasa**see**na*	**salmon**
палтус ***pal**toos*	**halibut**	сардины *sar**dee**niy*	**sardines**
омар *a**mar***	**lobster**	севрюга *siv**roo**ga*	**sevruga sturgeon**
окунь ***o**koon*	**perch**	шпроты ***shpro**tiy*	**sprats**
щука ***shchoo**ka*	**pike**	форель *far**yel***	**trout**
судак *soo**dak***	**pike-perch**	тунец *toon**yets***	**tuna**

Мясные блюда/*Myasniye blyooda*
Meat dishes

говядина с гарниром *gav**ya**deena sgar**neer**am*	**beef with vegetable garnish**	ветчина *vitchee**na***	**ham**
		почки ***poch**kee*	**kidneys**
гуляш с картофельем *gool**yash** skar**tof**ilyem*	**goulash and potatoes**	печёнка *pi**chon**ka*	**liver**

битки в томате *beetkee ftamatye*	**meatballs in tomato sauce**	с кровью *skrovyoo*	**rare**
баранина на вертеле *baraneena na virtelye*	**mutton on a skewer**	средне поджаренн-ый *sryedni podzharinniy*	**medium**
свинина с рисом *sveeneena sreesam*	**pork with rice**	хорошо прожар-енный *kharasho prazharinniy*	**well done**
котлеты *katlyetiy*	**rissoles/chops**	рагу *ragoo*	**stew**
бифштекс натуральный *beefshteks natooralniy*	**grilled steak**	телятина в сметане *tilyateena f smitanye*	**veal in sour cream**
филе/антрекот *feelay/antrekot*	**fillet/entrecote**		

Птица и дичь/*Pteetsa ee deech*
Poultry and game

цыплёнок жареный *tsiplyonak zhariniy*	**roast chicken**	гусь *goos*	**goose**
утка с яблоками *ootka syablakamee*	**duck with apples**	индейка *eendyeika*	**turkey**
		фазан *fazan*	**pheasant**
		рябчик *ryabcheek*	**grouse**

Фирменные блюда/*Firmyeniye blyooda*
Specialities

бефстрога-нов *befstroganof*	**Beef Stroganoff**	котлеты по-киевски *katlyetiy pa-kee-efski*	**Chicken Kiev**

цыплёнок табака *tsiy**plyon**ak taba**ka*** — **Chicken 'Tabaka' (spit roasted with garlic)**

кулебяка *koole**bya**ka* — **fish or meat pie**

чахохбили из кур *cha**khokh**bee-lee eez koor* — **Caucasian chicken casserole**

Cooking methods

печёный *pi**chon**iy* — **baked**

варёный *var**yon**iy* — **boiled**

жареный ***zhar**yeniy* — **fried/roast**

маринов-аный *maree**no**vaniy* — **marinaded**

отварной *at**var**noy* — **poached**

копчёный *kap**chon**iy* — **smoked**

паравой *para**voy*** — **steamed**

тушёный *too**shon**iy* — **stewed**

фарширов-анный *farshee**rov**an-niy* — **stuffed**

Десерт/*Disyert* Dessert

мороженое *ma**rozh**enoye* — **ice cream**

шоколад-ное *shaka**lat**noye* — **chocolate**

землянич-ное *zim**lyan**eech-noye* — **strawberry**

ванильное *va**neel**noye* — **vanilla**

компот *kam**pot*** — **fruit compote**

торт *tort* — **gateau**

яблочный пирог ***yab**lachniy pee**rok*** — **apple tart**

пирожное *pee**rozh**noye* — **pastry**

вареники *var**yen**eekee* — **dumplings**

блинчики с вареньем ***bleen**cheekee svar**yen**yem* — **pancakes with jam**

взбитые сливки *v**zbeet**iye **sleef**kee* — **whipped cream**

Drinks

- Note that you ask for spirits by weight in grams, unless you are buying the whole bottle.

Bring us a bottle/ glass ...	*Preeniseetye nam bootiylkoo/ stakan ...* Принесите нам бутылку/ стакан ...
... of red wine	*... krasnava veena* красного вина
... of white wine	*... byelava veena* белого вина
... of rosé wine	*... rozavava veena* розового вина
dry/sweet/sparkling wine	*sookhoye/slatkoye/ sheepoocheye veeno* сухое/сладкое/шипучее вино
beer (dark/light)	*peeva (tyomnoye/svyetloye)* пиво (тёмное/светлое)
champagne	*shampanskoye* шампанское
gin and tonic	*djeen stoneekam* джин с тоником
whisky	*veeskee* виски
neat	*natooralnoye* натуральное
on the rocks	*sa ldom* со льдом
brandy	*brendee* бренди
rum	*rom* ром
liqueur	*leekyor* ликёр

50 grams of cognac	*pitdis**yat** gram kanya**ka*** пятдесят грамм коньяка
100 grams of vodka	*sto gram **vot**kee* сто грамм водки
Cheers!	*Za **vashe** zda**rov**ye!* За ваше здоровье!

Paying

You may see:

Заплатите в кассе *Zapla**teet**ye f**kass**ye*	**Pay at the cash desk**

The bill, please	*Sshot, pa**zhal**asta* Счёт, пожалуйста
How much is that?	***Skol**ka smin**ya**?* Сколько с меня?
There is a mistake	*A**sheep**ka **fshot**ye* Ошибка в счёте
Please check the bill	*Prav**yer**tye, pa**zhal**asta, sshot* Проверьте, пожалуйста, счёт
I didn't order that	*Ya etava ni za**kaz**iyval* Я этого не заказывал
We ordered ...	*Miy zaka**zal**ee ...* Мы заказали ...
Do you take Intourist vouchers?	*Viy bir**yotye** ab**yed**inniye ta**lon**iy Eentoo**rees**ta?* Вы берёте обеденные талоны Интуриста?
Thank you, that was very nice	*Spaseeba, **biy**la **och**in **fkoos**na* Спасибо, было очень вкускно
Where are the toilets?	*Gdye zdyes twal**yet**iy?* Где здесь туалеты?

ENTERTAINMENT AND SPORT

Museums, galleries and exhibitions

- Opening times, shown on a plaque outside the building, are generally 10 or 11 am until 6 or 7 pm including Saturdays and Sundays. Museums are often shut on Mondays or Tuesdays, as well as one day a month for cleaning (санитарный день/ *saneetarniy dyen*). Last admissions are half an hour or an hour before closing time.
- Entrance charges are usually small, and organised foreign parties are often able to jump the queue for special exhibitions. Umbrellas, bags, etc., should be deposited in the cloakrooms.
- The taking of photographs is usually forbidden unless you have made special arrangements with the authorities.

How do I get to the ... museum?	*Kak praeetee f ... moozyei?* Как пройти в ... музей?
When does the museum open?	*Kagda atkriyvayetsa moozyei?* Когда открывается музей?
When does the art gallery close?	*Kagda zakriyvayetsa karteennaya galiryeya?* Когда закрывается картинная галерея?
Is the museum of fine arts open every day?	*Moozyei eezabrazeetyelniykh eeskoostv rabotayet kazhdiy dyen?* Музей изобразительных искусств работает каждый день?
What day is it shut?	*Kakoy viykhatnoy dyen?* Какой выходной день?
I want to visit ...'s house	*Ya khachoo pasyeteet dom-moozyei ...* Я хочу посетить дом-музей ...
What exhibition is on at the moment?	*Kakaya syeichas viystafka?* Какая сейчас выставка?
Where can I buy tickets for the exhibition?	*Gdye mozhna koopeet beelyetiy na viystafkoo?* Где можно купить билеты на выставку?

Where is ...?	*Gdye ...?* Где ...?
... the cash desk	*... kassa* касса
... the cloakroom	*... gardyirop* гардероб
... the (ladies/gents) toilet	*... (zhenskee/moozhskoy) twalyet* женский/мужской туалет

How much is ...?	***Skol**ka **stoy**eet ...?* Сколько стоит ...?
... an entrance ticket	*... fkhat**noy** beel**yet*** входной билет
... the catalogue	*... kata**lok*** каталог
... the museum guidebook	*... pootyeva**deet**yel pa moo**zye**yoo* путеводитель по музею

Do you have a reduction for students/children?
*Viy **dyel**ayetye **skeet**koo dlya stood**yen**taf/dit**yei**?*
Вы делаете скидку для студентов/детей?

Are you allowed to take photos?
*Zdyes **mozh**na fatagra**feer**avat?*
Здесь можно фотографировать?

Is there a guided tour?
*Yist lee eks**koor**seeya seks**koor**savodam?*
Есть ли экскурсия с экскурсоводом?

Where is the ... department/collection?
*Gdye at**dyel**/sa**bran**eeye ...?*
Где отдел/собрание ...?

Who is the artist/sculptor?
*Kto khoo**dozh**neek/skoolp**tor**?*
Кто художник/скульптор?

You may see:

МУЗЕЙ/КАССА РАБОТАЕТ ДО... *Moo**zyei**/**Kas**sa ra**bot**ayet da ...*	**Museum/Cash desk open until ...**
ВХОД *Fkhot*	**Entrance**
ВЫХОД ***Viy**khat*	**Exit**
КАССА ***Kas**sa*	**Cash desk**

ГАРДЕРОБ *Gardyi**rop***	**Cloakroom**
НАЧАЛО ОСМОТРА *Na**cha**la as**mo**tra*	**Start of the exhibition**
ФОТОГРАФИРОВАТЬ ЗАПРЕЩАЕТСЯ *Fatagra**feer**avat zaprish**cha**yetsa*	**No photographs**
М/Ж	**Ladies/Gents**

What's on?

- Theatres, concerts, ballet and opera performances are generally booked up months in advance, but some tickets are reserved for foreigners, and it is often possible to get good seats from the hotel service bureau or through Intourist. Failing this, one can also go to the theatre itself on the night in the hope of getting a return ticket (лишний билет/ ***leesh**nee beel**yet***), either from the box office or from private individuals.
- Theatre and ballet performances usually start at 7 pm and concerts at 7 or 7.30 pm. On Sundays and holidays, there may also be a matinee starting at midday. Coats and bags should be deposited in the cloakroom, and, at the theatre, cloakroom attendants hire out their own binoculars to members of the public for a small fee.
- In theatres, concert halls, etc., there is no entrance after the third bell has sounded, both at the beginning of the performance and after the interval. Smoking is not permitted in the auditorium. If you want to smoke, look for the designated smoking room (курительный зал/*kooree**ti**lniy zal*).
- Some theatres have extremely good buffets, where snacks and drinks are sold in the interval. You have to be quick off the mark in the best ones, such as

the Kremlin concert hall and Bolshoi Theatre in Moscow and the Kirov Theatre in Leningrad.

- Cinemas show films continuously, though each performance is separate, and the first showing is usually at 9 or 10 am. Tickets, which are numbered, can be bought the day before. Usherettes show you to your seat, but it is not permitted to enter after the main film has started.

What's on tonight?	*Shto eed**yot** si**vod**nya **vye**cheram?* Что идёт сегодня вечером?
I want to go ...	*Ya kha**choo** paee**tee** ...* Я хочу пойти ...
... to the theatre	*... fti**yatr*** в театр
... to the cinema	*... fkee**no*** в кино
... to the opera	*... **fop**yeroo* в оперу
... to the ballet	*... na bal**yet*** на балет
... to the circus	*... ftseerk* в цирк
I would like ...	*Ya khat**yel** biy* (**man**)/*khat**yela** biy* (**woman**) ... Я хотел/хотела бы ...
... to go to a concert	*... pas**loo**shat kant**syert*** послушать концерт
... to see a film/play	*... pasmat**ryet** feelm/**pye**soo* посмотреть фильм/пьесу
... to go to the puppet theatre	*... paee**tee** fkoo**kol**niy ti**yatr*** пойти в кукольный театр

... to go to the Bolshoi	*... paee**tee** fBal**shoy** ti**yatr*** пойти в Большой театр
... to go to the Kirov	*... paee**tee** f**Kee**rafskee ti**yatr*** пойти в Кировский театр

What do you recommend?	*Shto viy pasavye**too**yetye?* Что вы посоветуете?
Where is the (theatre) box office?	*Gdye (tiya**tral**naya) **kas**sa?* Где (театральная) касса?
When is the next showing?	*Kag**da slyed**ooyooshee sa**yans**?* Когда следующий сеанс?
Where can we go dancing?	*Gdye nam **mozh**na pa**tan**zivat?* Где нам можно потанцевать?

At the ticket office

- As well as at service bureaux, tickets can be bought direct from theatre/concert hall, etc., box offices and from underground and street kiosks. Look out on your ticket for the date, time of performance, row and seat number, and whether it's on the left, right or middle block.

Do you have any tickets ...?	*Oo vas yist beel**yet**iy ...?* У вас есть билеты ...?

... for today/tomorrow/ Saturday	*... na si**vod**nya/na **zaf**tra/na soo**bot**oo* на сегодня/на завтра/на субботу?
... for today's concert	*... na si**vod**nyashnee kants**yert*** на сегодняшний концерт
... for a matinee	*... na dnev**noy** spik**takl*** на дневной спектакль

Entertainment and sport

We want to book some tickets	*Miy khateem zakazat beelyetiy* Мы хотим заказать билеты
How much is a ticket?	*Skolka stoyeet adeen beelyet?* Сколько стоит один билет?

Two seats ..., please	*Dva myesta ..., pazhalasta* Два места ..., пожалуйста
... in the stalls	*... partyair* партер
... in the rear stalls	*... amfeetiyatr* амфитеатр
... in the dress circle	*... byeletazh* бельэтаж
... in the balcony	*... balkon* балкон
... in a box	*... lozha* ложа

Four tickets in the middle	*Chetiyrye beelyeta f sirideenye* Четыре билета в середине
on the left/right	*lyevaya/pravaya starana* левая/правая сторона
Can you show me on the plan?	*Pakazheetye na planye* Покажите на плане
Have you any other/better seats?	*Oo vas yist droogeeye/loochsheeye myesta?* У вас есть другие/лучшие места?
Have you anything cheaper?	*Oo vas yist shto-niboot padishevlye?* У вас есть что-нибудь подешевле?

What time does the performance begin/end?	*F**kato**ram cha**soo** nachee**na**yetsa/**kon**cheetsa spik**takl**?* В котором часу начинается/кончится спектакль?
Have you got a spare ticket?	*Nyet lee oo vas **leesh**nyeva beel**ye**ta?* Нет ли у вас лишнего билета?

You may hear:

*Vsye beel**ye**tiy **pro**daniy* Все билеты проданы	**All the tickets are sold**
*As**ta**las **tol**ka …* Осаталось только …	**We've only got … left**
***pyer**viy/f**ta**roy **ya**roos* первый/второй ярус	**first/second tier**

You may see:

ТЕАТРАЛЬНАЯ КАССА *Tiya**tral**naya **kas**sa*	**Theatre box office**
ПРОДАЖА БИЛЕТОВ НА СЕГОДНЯ *Pra**dazh**a beel**ye**taf na si**vod**nya*	**Sale of tickets for today**
ПРЕДВАРИТЕЛЬНАЯ ПРОДАЖА БИЛЕТОВ *Predva**reet**ilnaya pra**dazh**a beel**ye**taf*	**Advance ticket sales**
РЯД, МЕСТО, ЦЕНА *ryat, **mye**sta, tsye**na***	**Row, seat number, price**

In the theatre or cinema

Where is the cloakroom?	*Gdye gardyi**rop**?* Где гардероб?
A programme, please	*Pa**zhal**asta, prag**ram**moo* Пожалуйста, программу
How much is that?	***Skol**ka?* Сколько?
Please show us our seats	*Paka**zheet**ye, pa**zhal**asta, **nash**ee **myes**ta* Покажите, пожалуйста, наши места
How long is the interval?	*Kak **dol**ga **bood**yet an**trakt**?* Как долго будет антракт?
Where is the buffet/toilet?	*Gdye boof**yet**/twal**yet**?* Где буфет/туалет?
An ice cream, please	*Ma**rozh**enoye, pa**zhal**asta* Мороженое, пожалуйста

You may hear:

*Bee**nokl** **noozh**en?* Бинокль нужен?	**Do you want binoculars?**
*Vot vam nami**rok*** Вот вам номерок	**Here's your cloakroom ticket**
***Vash**ee beel**yet**iy, pa**zhal**asta* Ваши билеты, пожалуйста	**Your tickets, please**

You may see:

ВХОД В ЗРИТЕЛЬНЫЙ ЗАЛ *Fkhot v **zreet**yelniy zal*	**Entrance to auditorium**
ВЫХОД ***Viyk**hat*	**Exit**
НЕЛЬЗЯ КУРИТЬ *Nilz**ya** koo**reet***	**No smoking**

Excursions

- There are many special tours and excursions available for tourists, and details can be obtained from Intourist or the hotel service bureau.
- Many former churches have been beautifully restored or converted into museums. In churches where services are still held (действующие церкви/*dye-eest**voo**yooshcheeye tserk**vee***), people are expected to behave respectfully, and women should cover their heads with a scarf.

Where is the tourist bureau?	*Gdye byoo**ro** too**reez**ma?* Где бюро туризма?
What sights do you recommend?	*Shto biy viy passav**yet**avalee pasma**tryet**?* Что бы вы посоветовали посмотреть?
Is there an excursion ...?	*Yist lee ek**skoor**seeya ...?* Есть ли экскурсия ...?
... to the mountains/to the sea	*... f **go**riy/na **mor**ye* в горы/на море
... to the lake/round town	*... na **o**zyero/pa **gor**adooo* на озеро/по городу
I want to ...	*Ya kha**choo** ...* Я хочу ...
... visit the old town	*... pasye**teet** **star**iy **gor**at* посетить старый город
... look at the castle/palace	*... pasma**tryet** **za**mak/dvar**yets*** посмотреть замок/дворец
... see the church/mosque/ cemetery	*... pasma**tryet** **tser**kaf/mic**het**/ **klad**beeshchye* посмотреть церковь/ мечеть/кладбище

... see all the sights	*... asma**tryet** vsye dastapreemi**chat**ilnastee* осмотреть все достопримечательности
Do you have a map of the town?	*Oo vas yist plan **gor**ada?* У вас есть план города?
I would like to go ...	*Ya khat**yel** biy* (**man**)/*khat**yela** biy* (**woman**) *pra**yekh**at ...* Я хотел/хотела бы проехать ...
... to the zoo/to the botanical gardens	*... f zoo**park**/f bata**nee**cheskee sat* в зоопарк/в ботанический сад
... to the library/to the monastery	*... fbeebleeya**tyek**oo/fmanas**tiyr*** в библиотеку/в монастырь
How much is the trip?	***Skol**ka **stoy**eet pa**yezd**ka?* Сколько стоит поездка?
What time does the coach leave?	*Fka**tor**am cha**soo** atpravl**ya**yetsa af**to**boos?* В котором часу отправляется автобус?
Are there services at the church?	***E**ta dye-eest**voo**yooshchaya **tser**kaf?* Это действующая церковь?
Where is the entrance/exit?	*Gdye fkhot/**viy**khat?* Где вход/выход?
Can I take a photograph?	***Mozh**na fatagra**feer**avat?* Можно фотографировать?

You may see:

ВХОД БЕСПЛАТНЫЙ *Fxhot bis**plat**niy*	**Entrance free**
ЗАПАСНОЙ ВЫХОД *Zapas**noy** **viy**khat*	**Emergency exit**

Extra vocabulary

cathedral	*sa**bor**/khram* собор/храм	**monument**	***pam**yatneek* памятник
forest	*lyes* лес	**river**	*rye**ka*** река
fortress	***krye**past* крепость	**tomb**	*ma**gee**la* могила
fountain	*fon**tan*** фонтан	**tower**	***bash**nya* башня
gates	*vara**ta*** ворота	**walls**	*stye**niy*** стены

Sporting activities

- Most main cities have large, modern sports complexes and facilities, e.g. the Luzhniki Centre in Moscow and the Kirov Stadium in Leningrad. You can buy tickets to watch football, ice hockey, athletics, etc., either from the stadium, from metro kiosks or the hotel service bureau.
- Swimming is popular, and there are plenty of heated open-air pools. It is also possible to play tennis and go skating. Skis, skates and sledges can be hired for use in the Moscow and Leningrad parks.

Where's the nearest ...?	*Gdye bleez**ha**eeshee ...?* Где ближайший ...?
... swimming pool	*... **pla**vatyelniy bas**syein*** плавательный бассейн
... tennis court	*... **tyen**neesniy kort* теннисный корт
... sports complex	*... spar**tee**vniy **kom**pleks* спортивный комплекс
... stadium	*... stadee**on*** стадион
... skating rink	*... ka**tok*** каток

Where are the changing cubicles?	*Gdye ka**bee**niy dlya piri-adyeva**va**neeya?* Где кабины для переодевания?
Where can I play ...?	*Gdye zdyes **mozh**na ee**grat** f ...?* Где здесь можно играть в ...?
... football	*... foot**bol*** футбол
... golf	*... golf* гольф
... tennis	*... **tyen**nees* теннис
... volleyball	*... valyei**bol*** волейбол
... table tennis	*... peeng-pong* пинг-понг
... chess	*... **shakh**matiy* шахматы
I would like to ...	*Ya khat**yel*** (**man**)/*khat**yel**a* (**woman**) *biy ...* Я хотел/хотела бы ...
... go skiing	*... kha**deet** na **liy**zhakh* ходить на лыжах
... go skating	*... ka**tat**sa na kan**kakh*** кататься на коньках
... go cycling	*... ka**tat**sa na vyelasee**pyed**ye* кататься на велосипеде
... go for a troika (sleigh) ride	*... ka**tat**sa na **tro**eekye* кататься на тройке
Where can we hire ...?	**Gdye** ***mozh**na vzyat na**pro**kat ...?* Где можно взять напрокат ...?

... skis	... ***liy**zhee* лыжи
... ski boots	... ***liyzh**niye ba**teen**kee* лыжные ботинки
... skates	... ***kon**kee* коньки
... a sledge	... ***san**ee* сани
... tennis rackets	... ***tyen**neesniye rak**yet**kee* теннисные ракетки
... balls	... ***myach**ee* мячи

I am keen on ...	*Ya zanee**may**oos ...* Я занимаюсь ...
... athletics	... *at**lyet**eekoy* атлетикой
... gymnastics	... *geem**nast**eekoy* гимнастикой
... ice hockey	... *khak**kyei*** хоккей
... fishing	... ***riy**bnoy **lof**koy* рыбной ловкой

I'm very fond of ...	*Ya **och**in lyoob**lyoo** ...* Я очень люблю ...
... boxing	... *boks* бокс
... climbing	... *alpeen**eezm*** альпинизм
... horse-racing	... *skach**kee*** скачки
... playing cards	... *ee**grat** **fkar**tiy* играть в карты

Where can I buy tickets?	*Gdye* ***mozh****na koo****peet*** *beel****yet****iy?* Где можно купить билеты?
When does it begin/end?	*Kag****da*** *on nachee****na****yetsa/* ***kon****cheetsa?* Когда он начинается/ кончится?
Two tickets, please	*Dva beel****yet****a, pa****zhal****asta* Два билета, пожалуйста
What is the score?	*K****akoy*** *sshot?* Какой счёт?
Who won the match/ competition?	*Kto* ***viy****eegral match/ saryevna****van****eeye?* Кто выиграл матч/ соревнование?

Other interests

I'm very fond of music	*Ya* ***och****in lyoob****lyoo*** ***moo****ziykoo* Я очень люблю музыку
I play the ...	*Ya eeg****ra****yoo na ...* Я играю на ...
... piano/violin	*... peea****nee****na/****skreep****kye* пианино/скрипке
... guitar/flute	*... gee****tar****ye/****flye****itye* гитаре/флейте
I'm interested in ...	*Ya eentyerye****soo****yoos ...* Я интересуюсь ...
... photography	*... fata****graf****eeyei* фотографией
... architecture	*... arkheetyek****too****roy* архитектурой

At the seaside

How do we get to the beach?	*Kak da**brat**sa da **plya**zha?* Как добраться до пляжа?
Is it far?	***E**ta dali**ko**?* Это далеко?
Can we swim here?	*Zdyes **mozh**na koo**pat**sa?* Здесь можно купаться?
Is it safe for children?	*Koo**pat**sa byeza**pas**na dlya dit**yei**?* Купаться безопасно для детей?
Can I hire ...?	***Mozh**na vzyat na**pro**kat ...?* Можно взять напрокат ...?
... a canopy/deckchair/ beach hut	*... tyent/shez**long**/ koo**pal**nyoo* тент/шезлонг/купальню
... a rowing boat/ speedboat	*... **gryeb**nooyoo **lot**koo/ glees**yair*** гребную лодку/ глиссер
... a yacht/pedalo	*... **yakh**too/**vod**niy vyelasee**pyet*** яхту/водный велосипед
... an umbrella/water skis	*... **zon**teek/**vod**niye **liy**zhee* зонтик/водные лыжи
... a windsurfer/fishing tackle	*... **syer**feeng/riyba**lov**niye **snas**tee* серфинг/рыболовные снасти
How much is it per hour?	***Skol**ka **stoy**eet fchas?* Сколько стоит в час?

You may see:

КУПАТЬСЯ ЗАПРЕЩЕНО
*Koo**pat**sa zaprishchi**no***

No swimming

HEALTH

- It is advisable to take out medical insurance, to cover hospital treatment and in case you need to be flown home. However, although medicines on prescription have to be paid for, health treatment is free in the Soviet Union. There are no GPs and the health service is run on a system of polyclinics. There is a special clinic for foreigners in Moscow (Gruzinsky Pereulok 3, Korpus 2).
- Many Western medicines do not exist in the Soviet Union, and visitors who rely on certain drugs should take an adequate supply with them. In case of illness, the hotel will call the duty doctor who is equipped to give simple injections and supply prescriptions for proprietary drugs.
- See also **Chemist's** on page 125.

Medical problems

I don't feel very well	*Ya **plokh**a sib**ya** **choost**vooyoo* Я плохо себя чувстсвую
He/She doesn't feel very well	*On/A**na** **plokh**a **choost**vooyet sib**ya*** Он/Она плохо чувствует себя
I want to make an appointment with the doctor	*Ya kha**choo** zapee**sat**sa na pree**yom** k **vrach**oo* Я хочу записаться на приём к врачу
I need a doctor who speaks English	*Mnye **noo**zhen vrach, ka**tor**iy gava**reet** pa-an**glee**skee* Мне нужен врач, который говорит по-английски
Call a doctor urgently	***Viy**zaveetye **vrach**a, paskar**ye**ye* Вызовите врача, поскорее
Call an ambulance!	***Viy**zaveetye **skor**ooyoo **pom**ashch!* Вызовите скорую помощь!

Symptoms

I've got ...	*Oo min**ya** ba**leet** ...* У меня болит ...
He's got/She's got ...	*Oo nye**vo**/oo nye**yo** ba**leet** ...* У него/у неё болит ...
... a headache	*... gala**va*** голова
... a sore throat	*... **gor**la* горло
... stomach ache	*... zhi**lood**ak* желудок
... a bad back/arm/leg	*... spee**na**/roo**ka**/na**ga*** спина/рука/нога
... a pain in the chest/side	*... groot/bok* грудь/бок

Health

It hurts here	*Oo min**ya** ba**leet** zdyes* У меня болит здесь
I feel sick	*Min**ya** tash**neet*** Меня тошнит
I've been sick	*Min**ya** **rvyot*** Меня рвёт
I've got a temperature/ a bad pain	*Oo min**ya** timpera**too**ra/ **os**traya bol* У меня температура/ острая боль
I can't eat/sleep	*Ya ni ma**goo** yist/spat* Я не могу есть/спать
I feel short of breath/dizzy	*Oo min**ya** **adiysh**ka/ **kroo**zheetsa gala**va*** У меня одышка/кружится голова
He's/She's fainted	*Oo nye**vo**/Oo nye**yo** **op**marak* У него/У неё обморок

I've got/He's got/She's got ...	*Oo min**ya**/Oo nye**vo**/Oo nye**yo** ...* У меня/У него/У неё ...

... a cold/a cough	*... nas**mork**/**kash**el* насморк/кашель
... flu/migraine	*... greep/**mee**gren* грипп/мигрень
... diarrhoea/constipation	*... pa**nos**/za**por*** понос/запор
... indigestion/food poisoning	*... ras**stroy**stva zhi**loot**ka/ atrav**lyen**eeye* расстройство желудка/ отравление
... a rash/a swelling	*... siyp/**op**ookhal* сыпь/опухоль
... a cut/a burn	*... par**yez**/a**zhok*** порез/ожог
... a boil/cramp	*... foo**roon**kool/**soo**daraga* фурункул/судорога

... an insect bite/a nose bleed	... *oo**koos** nasi**ko**mava/krava-ti**chen**eeye eez **no**sa* укус насекомого/ кровотечение из носа
... hay fever/sunstroke	... *sin**na**ya leekha**rat**ka/ **sol**nichniy oo**dar*** сенная лихорадка/ солнечный удар

I've got something in my eye	*Oo min**ya** shto-ta f gla**zoo*** У меня что-то в глазу
I've cut my leg	*Ya par**ye**zal* (**man**)/*par**ye**zala* (**woman**) *na**goo*** Я порезал/порезала ногу
I've burnt my hand	*Ya ap**zhok*** (**man**)/*abazh**gla*** (**woman**) ***roo**koo* Я обжёг/обожгла руку
I've hurt my finger	*Ya para**neel*** (**man**)/*para**nee**la* (**woman**) ***pal**yits* Я поранил/поранила палец
I fell	*Ya oo**pal*** (**man**)/*oo**pal**a* (**woman**) Я упал/упала

I think I've ...	***Doo**mayoo, shto ya ...* Думаю, что я ...

... broken my leg	... *sla**mal*** (**man**)/*sla**mal**a* (**woman**) *sib**ye** na**goo*** сломал/сломала себе ногу
... sprained my ankle	... *rastya**nool*** (**man**)/ *rastya**nool**a* (**woman**) *sib**ye** la**diyzh**koo* растянул/растянула себе лодыжку
... dislocated my shoulder	... ***viy**veekhnool* (**man**)/*-noola* (**woman**) *sib**ye** pli**cho*** вывихнул/-нула себе плечо

Health

I've got a pain in my ... — *Oo min**ya** ba**leet** ...* У меня болит ...

Parts of the body

ankle	*la**diysh**ka*	лодышка
arm	*roo**ka***	рука
back	*spee**na***	спина
blood	*krof*	кровь
bone	*kost*	кость
cheek	*shchi**ka***	щека
chest	*groot*	грудь
chin	*padba**ro**dak*	подбородок
ear (ears)	***oo**kha (**oo**shee)*	ухо (уши)
elbow	***lo**kat*	локать
eye (eyes)	*glaz (gla**za**)*	глаз (глаза)
face	*leet**so***	лицо
finger	***pal**yits*	палец
foot	*na**ga***	нога
forehead	*lop*	лоб
hair	***vo**lasiy*	волосы
hand	*roo**ka***	рука
head	*gala**va***	голова
heart	***sert**se*	сердце
hip	*bid**ro***	бедро
joint	*soos**taf***	сустав
knee	*kal**ye**na*	колено
leg	*na**ga***	нога
lip	*goo**ba***	губа
mouth	*rot*	рот
muscle	***miysh**tsa*	мышца
neck	***she**ya*	шея
nose	*nos*	нос
rib	*rib**ro***	ребро
shoulder	*pli**cho***	плечо
skin	***ko**zha*	кожа
stomach	*zhi**loo**dak*	желудок
tongue	*ya**ziyk***	язык
wrist	*zap**ya**stye*	запястье

You may hear:

*Shto oo vas ba**leet**?* Что у вас болит?	**Where does it hurt?**
*Dav**no** oo vas ba**leet**?* Давно у вас болит?	**Has it been hurting long?**
*Mnye **na**da vas asmat**ryet*** Мне надо вас осмотреть	**I'll have to examine you**
*Pa**zhal**asta, raz**dyen**tyes/ la**zheet**yes* Пожалуйста, раздентесь/ложитесь	**Undress/Lie down, please**
*Diy**sheet**ye **gloop**zhe/ **Kash**lyaneetye* Дышите глубже/ Кашляните	**Breathe deeply/Cough**
*Zdyes **bol**na* Здесь больно?	**Does this hurt?**
*Ka**koye** li**kar**stva viy preenee**may**etye?* Какое лекарство вы принимаете?	**What (medicine/pills) are you taking?**

Medical conditions

I'm …	*Ya …* Я …
… asthmatic	*… ast**ma**teek* астматик
… diabetic	*… deea**byet**eek* диабетик
… epileptic	*… epeel**yep**teek* эпилептик

I've got ...	*Oo minya* У меня ...
... a heart condition	*... **bol**noye **sert**se* больное сердце
... high/low blood pressure	*... viy**sok**oye/**neez**koye kravya**noye** dav**lyen**eeye* высокое/низкое кровяное давление
... a stomach ulcer	*... **yaz**va zhi**loot**ka* язва желудка
I had a heart attack/ stroke recently	*Ya nidav**no** pirin**yos*** **(man)**/ *pirinis**la*** **(woman)** *sird**yech**niy **prees**toop/een**farkt*** Я недавно перенёс/ перенесла сердечный приступ/инфаркт
I'm allergic to penicillin	*Oo min**ya** all**yer**geeya na pineetsee**leen*** У меня аллергия на пенициллин
I'm taking tablets for ...	*Ya preenee**ma**yoo tabl**yet**kee dlya ...* Я принимаю таблетки для ...
I need a prescription for ...	*Mnye **noozh**en rits**yept** dlya ...* Мне нужен рецепт для ...
I'm pregnant	*Ya bir**yem**inna* Я беременна

Diagnosis and remedy

You may hear:

*Oo vas/Oo nye**vo**/Oo nye**yo** **kazh**itsa ...* У вас/У него/У неё кажется ...	**I think you've got/He's got/She's got ...**

... ***pree**stoop appindeet**seeta*** приступ аппендицита	**... appendicitis**
... *bran**kheet*** бронхит	**... bronchitis**
... *likha**rat**ka* лихорадка	**... a fever**
... ***tresh**cheena* трещина	**... a fracture**
... *greep* грипп	**... flu**
... *gas**treet*** гастрит	**... gastritis**
... *griyz**ha*** грыжа	**... a hernia**
... *peetsi**vo**ye atrav**lyen**eeye* пицевое отравление	**... food poisoning**
... *een**fekt**seeya* инфекция	**... an infection**
... *pnevma**nee**ya* пневмания	**... pneumonia**
... *tanzeel**leet*** тонзиллит	**... tonsillitis**

*Neeche**vo** sir**yoz**nava* Ничего серьёзного	**It's nothing serious**
*Viy dalzh**niy** liz**ha**t f past**yel*** Вы должны лежать в постель	**You must stay in bed**
... *dva-tree dnya* два-три дня	**... for two to three days**
*Vam **na**da f palee**klee**neekoo/ f bal**neet**soo* Вам надо в поликлинику/ в больницу	**You need to go to the polyclinic/to hospital**

*Ya vam **sdyel**ayoo …* Я вам сделаю …	**I'm going to give you …**
*… rit**sept*** рецепт	**… a prescription**
*… oo**kol*** укол	**… an injection**
*… pree**veef**koo* прививку	**… an innoculation**
*… **myes**tniy nar**koz*** местный наркоз	**… a local anaesthetic**
*… rint**gyen*** рентген	**… an X-ray**
*Ya **pro**peeshoo vam li**kar**stva/tabl**yet**kee* Я пропишу вам лекарство/таблетки	**I'm going to prescribe some medicine/tablets**
*… anteebee**o**teekee/balye-ootal**ya**ooshcheye* антибиотики/болеутоляющее	**… antibiotics/painkillers**
*Ya kha**choo** s**dye**lat ana**leez*** Я хочу сделать анализ	**I want to do some tests**
*Ya vas oo**vee**zhoo **zaf**tra/**chye**riz dva dnya* Я вас увижу завтра/через два дня	**I'll see you again tomorrow/in two days**

You may see:

БОЛЬНИЦА *Bal**neet**sa*	**Hospital**
ПОЛИКЛИНИКА *Paleek**leen**eeka*	**Polyclinic**

Dentist and optician

I need a dentist	*Mnye **noo**zhen zoop**noy** vrach* Мне нужен зубной врач
I've ...	*Oo min**ya** ...* У меня ...
... got toothache	*... zoop**na**ya bol* зубная боль
... lost a filling	*... **viy**pala **plom**ba* выпала пломба
... broken a tooth/bridge/my appliance	*... sla**mal**sa zoob/most/ prat**yez*** сломался зуб/мост/ протез
I think I've got an abscess	*Oo min**ya** **kazh**itsa na**riyv*** У меня кажется нарыв
My gums hurt	*Oo min**ya** **dyos**niy bal**yat*** У меня дёсны болят
Can you give me a temporary filling?	***Mozh**na pas**ta**veet **vryem**innooyoo **plom**boo?* Можно поставить временную пломбу?
Can you mend my appliance/ bridge temporarily?	***Mozh**na pachee**neet** **vryem**enna prat**yez**/most?* Можно починить временно протез/мост?
Please don't take the tooth out	*Pa**zhal**asta, ni oodal**ya**eetye **e**tat zoop* Пожалуйста, не удаляйте этот зуб
I've broken my glasses	*Ya raz**beel*** **(man)***/raz**beel**a* **(woman)** *ach**kee*** Я разбил/разбила очки
I'm short-sighted/ long-sighted	*Oo min**ya** bleeza**rook**ast/ dalna**zork**ast* У меня близорукость/ дадьнозоркость

TRAVEL

Asking your way

For finding your way around, maps can be bought at street kiosks for around 30 kopecks. In addition, you can get information such as an address or telephone number, or written instructions as to how to get from A to B, from a Справочное Бюро/***Sprav****achnoye* *Byoo***ro*** or Справка/***Spraf****ka* (Information Office), found on many street corners. There is a fee of a few kopecks.

How do I get there? (on foot)	*Kak too**da** praee**tee**?* Как туда пройти?
How do I get there? (by transport)	*Kak too**da** pra**yekh**at?* Как туда проехать?

I'm lost	*Ya zabloo**deel**sa* (**man**)/ *ya zabloo**deel**as* (**woman**) Я заблудился/я заблудилась
Excuse me, how do I get ... ?	*Pras**teet**ye, kak praee**tee** ...?* Простите, как пройти ...?
... to the hotel/theatre/bank	*... f gas**teen**eetsoo/ti**yatr**/ bank* в гостиницу/театр/ банк
... to the metro station/ post office	*... na **stant**seeyoo mi**tro**/ **poch**too* на станцию метро/ почту
How do I get to the town centre?	*Kak pa**past** f tsentr **gor**ada?* Как попасть в центр города?
Can I get there on foot?	***Mozh**na too**da** praee**tee** pish**kom**?* Можно туда пройти пешком?
Do you know where ... is?	*Viy ni **zna**yetye gdye na**khod**eetsa ...?* Вы не знаете где находится ...?
... the library/swimming pool	*... beebleea**tye**ka/bass**yein*** библиотека/бассейн
... the museum/stadium	*... mooz**yei**/stadee**on*** музей/стадион
... the taxi rank/bus stop	*... sta**yan**ka tak**see**/asta**nof**ka af**to**boosa* стоянка такси/ остановка автобуса
Show me on the map	*Paka**zheet**ye na **kar**tye* Покажите на карте

Travel

I want to go …

*Ya kha**choo** praee**tee** …*
Я хочу пройти …

… to Red Square

*… na **Kras**nooyoo **plosh**chat*
на Красную площадь

… to the Nevsky Prospekt

*… na **Nyef**skee pras**pyekt***
на Невский проспект

… to Gorky Street

*… na **oo**leetsoo **Gor**kava*
на улицу Горького

… to the Bolshoi/to the Kirov Theatre

*… fBal**shoy**/**fKee**rafskee ti**yatr***
в Большой/в Кировский театр

Draw me a plan of how to get there

*Naree**soo**yetye, pa**zhal**asta, kak too**da** praee**tee***
Нарисуете, пожалуйста, как туда пройти

Am I going the right way for the restaurant 'Armenia'?

*Ya **pra**veelna ee**doo** f rista**ran** Ar**myen**eeya?*
Я правильно иду в ресторан "Армения"?

Can you tell me where the information office is please?

*Ska**zheet**ye, pa**zhal**asta, gdye **sprav**achnoye byoo**ro**?*
Скажите, пожалуйста, где справочное бюро?

What's the name of this street/square?

*Kak naziy**va**yetsa **e**ta **oo**leetsa/**plosh**chat?*
Как называется эта улица/площадь?

You may hear:

*Von tam, na**prot**eef*
Вон там, напротив

There it is, opposite

***E**ta dali**ko**/nidali**ko**/**blee**zka/**rya**dam s …*
Это далеко/недалеко/близко/рядом с …

It's a long way/not far/near/next to …

*Ee**deet**ye **prya**ma/a**brat**na* Идите прямо/обратно	**Go straight on/back**
*Pavyer**neet**ye na**prava**/ **nalyeva*** Поверните направо/ налево	**Turn right/left**
*Viy oo**vee**deetye ye**vo** **slyeva*** Вы увидите его слева	**You'll see it on the left**
*Vam **loosh**che **yekh**at na **mitro*** Вам лучше ехать на метро	**You'd better take the metro**
*Vam **na**da syest na trall**yei**boos* Вам надо сесть на троллейбус	**You need to take a trolleybus**

You may see:

СТОП *stop*	**Stop**
СТОЙТЕ ***sto**eetye*	**Wait**
ИДИТЕ *ee**deet**ye*	**Cross now**
БЕРЕГИСЬ АВТОМОБИЛЯ *byeri**gees** aftama**beel**ya*	**Beware of cars**
ПЕРЕХОД *piri**khot***	**Crossing**

Taking a taxi

- Taxis are identified by the checked stripe on the side or roof, and a green light is displayed in the window if the taxi is free. They can be found at a rank (стоянка такси/*sta**yan**ka tak**see***), recognisable by the sign of a T, or hailed in the street. Although all are metered, they may charge tourists inflated rates, or refuse to go to certain destinations unless a high fee has been negotiated. Sometimes, a box of Western cigarettes is a helpful inducement.

- Hotels will book taxis in advance, e.g. to take visitors to the theatre.
- In many towns there is a minibus taxi service (маршрутные такси/*marsh**root**niye tak**see***) which follows specific routes and is very cheap. These taxis will also stop on demand. A flat-rate fare of 15 kopecks operates.

Taxi!	*Tak**see**!* Такси!
Are you free?	*Viy sva**bod**niy?* Вы свободны?
To the ... hotel, please	*F gas**teen**eetsoo ..., pa**zhal**asta* В гостиницу ..., пожалуйста
To the ... restaurant/to the theatre	*F rista**ran** .../ftii**yatr*** В ресторан .../в театр
To Gorky Street/to Prospekt Mira	*Na **oo**leetsoo **Gor**kava/na pras**pyekt** **Mee**ra* На улицу Горького/на проспект Мира
To the airport/to the station	*F aera**port**/na vak**zal*** В аэропорт/на вокзал
To the British/American Embassy	*F Bree**tan**skoye/Amiree**kan**skoye pa**sol**stva* В Британское/Американское посольство
I'm in a hurry	*Ya spi**shoo*** Я спешу
I want to go to this address	*Ya kha**choo** pa**past** pa **e**tamoo a**dryes**oo* Я хочу попасть по этому адресу
Is it far?	*Eta dali**ko**?* Это далеко?

How long will it take?	***Skol**ka **vryemi**nee zaeem**yot** pa**yezd**ka?* Сколько времени займёт поездка?
How much will it cost?	***Skol**ka **bood**yet **stoy**eet?* Сколько будет стоить?
Can you write it down?	*Napee**sheet**ye, pa**zhal**asta* Напишите, пожалуйста
Wait a minute, please. I'm coming back	*Padazh**deet**ye, pa**zhal**asta. Ya vyer**noos*** Подождите, пожалуйста. Я вернусь

You may hear:

*Koo**da** vam?* Куда вам?	**Where to?**
*S vas ... roob**lyei*** С вас ... рублей	**That'll be ... roubles**

Bus, trolleybus, tram and metro

- Buses, trolleybuses, etc., run from 5 or 5.30 am until 1 am. A flat-rate fare of 5 kopecks is paid into a box, and a ticket torn off the roll. If the bus is crowded, fares are passed along to the person nearest the box. Tickets must be validated in the date-stamping machine (компостер/*kam**post**yair*) which is fixed to the wall. Buses, trolleybuses, etc., should be entered from the rear or middle doors. In major cities, books of ten tickets can be bought from the driver or street kiosks, and weekly or monthly travelcards valid on all forms of transport are also available. You can be fined for travelling without a ticket if an inspector (usually in plain clothes) catches you.

- Many major cities also have metro (underground) systems. The one in Moscow is famous for its luxurious stations, some with chandeliers, mosaics, marble and bronze sculptures, and it is worth a special trip just to visit them.
- Metro stations can be recognised by a capital M, illuminated at night, and trains run from 6 am until 1 am (5 am until 2 am on some public holidays). Here too a flat-rate fare of 5 kopecks operates. Change can be obtained from a change machine (размен/*raz**myen***) or from the cash window (касса/***kas**sa*) and the 5-kopeck piece fed into the automatic gate which then allows you to pass. Metro maps can be obtained from kiosks and are prominently displayed in all stations, and the system is not difficult to follow. Some stations have display stands in which your best route to a place is automatically illuminated.
- Station names on platforms are not as well signed as in the UK, and all signs are in Cyrillic so it is advisable to listen out for the announcements. At every station, the name of the stop and the one after it are given.

Where's the nearest ...?	*Gdye bleez**ha**eeshaya ...?* Где ближайшая?
... bus/trolleybus stop	*... asta**nof**ka af**to**boosa/ trall**yei**boosa* остановка автобуса/ троллейбуса
... tram stop/metro station	*... asta**nof**ka tram**va**ya/ **stant**seeya mi**tro*** остановка трамвая/ станция метро
How often do the buses/fixed-route taxis run?	*Kak **chas**ta **khod**yat af**to**boosiy/marsh**root**niye tak**see**?* Как часто ходят автобусы/ маршрутные такси?

What number do I need for the town centre/hotel?

*Ka**koy** **nom**ir f tsentr **gor**ada/gas**teen**eetsoo?*
Какой номер в центр города/гостиницу?

Which number goes to the museum/cathedral?

*Ka**koy** **nom**ir eed**yot** **da** mooz**ye**ya/sa**bor**a?*
Какой номер идёт до музея/собора?

Does this bus go to ...?

*Eed**yot** lee **e**tat af**to**boos da ...?*
Идёт ли этот автобус до ...?

Does this train go to ... station?

*Eed**yot** lee **e**tat **po**yezd da **stant**see ...?*
Идёт ли этот поезд до станции ...?

How many stops?

***Skol**ka asta**no**vak?*
Сколько остановок?

Do I have to change?

*Mnye **na**da **dyel**at piri**sat**koo?*
Мне надо делать пересадку?

Where do I buy a ticket?

*Gdye **mozh**na koo**peet** beel**yet**?*
Где можно купить билет?

How much is it?

***Skol**ka **stoy**eet pra**yezd**?*
Сколько стоит проезд?

A book of bus tickets, please

***Da**eetye mnye **kneezh**koo, pa**zhal**asta*
Дайте мне книжку, пожалуйста

Please pass my (bus) voucher along

*Piri**da**eetye ta**lon**, pa**zhal**asta*
Передайте талон, пожалуйста

Will you tell me when to get off?

*Viy mnye **ska**zhete, kag**da** mnye **viy**khadeet?*
Вы мне скажете, когда мне выходить?

What's this station?

*Ka**ka**ya eta **stant**seeya?*
Какая эта станция?

What's the next station?	*K**a**kaya **slyed**ooyooshchaya **stant**seeya?* Какая следующая станция?

You may hear:

*Vam **noozh**na **viy**khadeet na **slyed**ooyooshchei* Вам нужно выходить на следующей	**You have to get off at the next stop**
*Vam **noozh**na **dyel**at piri**sat**koo f ...* Вам нужно делать пересадку в ...	**You have to change at ...**
*Astar**ozh**na, **dvyer**ee zakriy**va**yootsa* Осторожно, двери закрываются	**Take care, doors closing**
***Slyed**ooyooshchaya **stant**seeya ...* Следующая станция ...	**The next station is ...**
Po**yezd **dal**she ni eed**yot Поезд дальше не идёт	**The train doesn't go any further**
***Pros**ba asva**bod**eet va**gon**iy* Просьба освободить вагоны	**Please leave the train**

You may see:

РАЗМЕН *Raz**myen***	**Change**
К ПОЕЗДАМ *K payez**dam***	**To the trains**
ПЕРЕХОД *Piri**khot***	**Connections**
ВЫХОД В ГОРОД ***Viy**khat f gorat*	**Exit to the town**
НЕ ПРИСЛОНЯТЬСЯ *Ni preeslan**yat**sa*	**Do not lean against**

Driving

- It is becoming more common for tourists to take their own cars to the Soviet Union. Motorists who wish to do so should contact Intourist well in advance to plan their route and fix overnight stops on approved Intourist routes.
- It is now possible to hire a car in major cities, and you can also hire a car with a driver. Your hotel service bureau will arrange this for you.
- Driving is on the right, and multi-lane roads are not always clearly marked so extra care should be taken. Do not cross a single unbroken central line. Priority is to the right, and motorists must give way to trams and buses. Road signs are international, and parking is not difficult, as even in main cities there are few restrictions.
- It is compulsory for drivers and front-seat passengers to wear seat-belts. Drinking and driving is punishable by a fine.
- The speed limit is 60 kph (37 mph) in town, 90 kph (56 mph) elsewhere. Country roads are mainly dual carriageways with a central reservation and there are few motorways. Roads are patrolled by the Russian traffic police, the ГАИ (*GAI*). Driving in the Soviet Union can be hazardous as road surfaces are extremely poor.

Hiring a car

I need to order a car

Mnye ***noozh****na zaka****zat*** *ma****shee****noo*
Мне нужно заказать машину

I want to hire a car

*Ya kha****choo*** *vzyat ma****shee****noo na****prok****at*
Я хочу взять машину напрокат

How much does it cost for a day?

Skol*ka* ***stoy****eet* ***za*** *dyen?*
Сколько стоит за день?

Is petrol included in the price?	*Bin**zeen** **fklyoo**chen f tsye**noo**?* Бензин включен в цену?
Is insurance included?	*Stra**khof**ka fklyooche**na**?* Страховка включена?
Here is ...	*Vot ...* Вот ...
... my passport	*... moy **pas**part* мой паспорт
... my (international) driving licence	*... maee (mizhdoonna**rod**niye) pra**va*** мои (международные) права
Can I leave the car at the hotel?	***Mozh**na asta**veet** ma**sheen**oo f gas**teen**eetsye* Можно оставить машину в гостинице?
Show me how it works	*Poka**zheet**ye mnye kak a**na** ra**bot**ayet* Покажите мне, как она работает

Driving around

I want to go to ...	*Ya kha**choo** pra**yekh**at da ...* Я хочу проехать до ...
In which direction is ...?	*F ka**kom** napravl**yen**ee'ee ...?* В каком направлении ...?
Am I going the right way for ...?	*Ya **pra**veelna **ye**doo k ...?* Я правильно еду к ...?
Does this road go to ...?	***E**ta da**ro**ga vid**yot** k ...?* Это дорога ведёт к ...?
Can you show me on the map?	*Viy **mozh**etye mnye paka**zat** na **kart**ye?* Вы можете мне показать на карте?

Where's there a car park?	*Gdye zdyes sta**yan**ka aftama**beel**yei?* Где здесь стоянка автомобилей?
Can I park here?	***Mozh**na pas**ta**veet aftama**beel** zdyes?* Можно поставить автомобиль здесь?
Is it far to the service station/petrol station?	*Aftas**tant**seeya/Benzaka**lon**ka da**lik**o?* Автостанция/ бензоколонка далеко?
Ten/twenty/thirty litres of petrol, please	***Dye**syat/**dvat**sat/**treed**sat **leet**raf bin**zee**na, pa**zhal**asta* Десять/двадцать/тридцать литров бензина, пожалуйста
Fill the tank	*Na**pol**neetye bak* Наполните бак

You may see:

ПРОЕЗД ВОСПРЕЩЁН *pra**yezd** vasprish**chon***	**No entry**
ОДНОСТОРОННЕЕ ДВИЖЕНИЕ *adnasta**ron**yeye dvee**zhen**eeye*	**One-way street**
ОБЪЕЗД *Ab**yezt***	**Diversion**
ПЕШЕХОДНЫЙ ПЕРЕХОД *Pishi**khod**niy piri**khot***	**Pedestrian crossing**

Problems with the car

- If your car breaks down, you could be in trouble, as Soviet garages are not equipped for foreign makes. It is therefore sensible to take plenty of spare parts with you, and have your car checked thoroughly before you set out. It is also advisable to take such things as a spare petrol can, oil can, plus your own oil, battery top-up, antifreeze, brake oil, etc., and an extensive tool kit.

My car has broken down	*Oo minya slamalas masheena* У меня сломалась машина
I've run out of petrol	*Oo minya koncheelsa binzeen* У меня кончился бензин
I've got a flat tyre	*Oo minya lopnoola sheena* У меня лопнула шина
Send for/phone a mechanic	*Viyzaveetye/Pazaveetye mikhaneeka* Вызовите/Позовите механика
Can you send a breakdown lorry?	*Mozhna paslat groozaveek, shtobiy minya vzyat na bookseer?* Можно послать грузовик, чтобы меня взять на буксир?
Can you ...?	*Mozhna ...?* Можно ...?
... change the wheel	*... zamyeneet kalyeso* заменить колесо
... change this bulb	*... zamyeneet etoo lampoo* заменить эту лампу
... recharge the battery	*... zaryadeet akkoomoolyatar* зарядить аккумулятор
The tyre pressure needs checking	*Nada pravyereet davlyeneeye f sheenakh* Надо проверить давление в шинах
I don't know what's the matter	*Ya ni znayoo tochna f chom prablyema* Я не знаю точно в чём проблема

There's something wrong with ...	*... ni f par***yat***kye* не в порядке
... the accelerator/the carburettor	*aksili***rat***ar/karbyoo***ra***tar ...* акселератор/ карбюратор
... the brakes/the clutch	***tor****maza/stsip***lyen***eeye ...* тормоза/сцепление
... the engine/the fan belt	***mot****ar/vinteelyatsee***yon***niy ri***myen** ...* мотор/вентиляционный ремень
... the gears/the ignition	***skor****astee/zazhee***gan***eeye ...* скорости/зажигание
... the headlights/the windscreen wipers	***far****iy/stiklo-achees***teet***yelee ...* фары/стеклоочистители
... the plugs/the steering wheel	*sv***icha** *zazhee***gan***eeya/rool ...* свеча зажигания/руль

Something is burning/ overheating/smells	*Shto-ta* ***gor****eet/pirigri***vay***etsa/* ***pakh****nyet* Что-то горит/ перегревается/пахнет
There's a noise somewhere	*Gdye-to* ***shoom****eet* Где-то шумит
Can you mend it?	*Viy* ***mozh****itye pachee***neet***?* Вы можете починить?
When will the car be ready?	*Kag***da** *ma***shee***na* ***bood****yet ga***tova***?* Когда машина будет готова?
I have to get to ... today	*Mnye* ***na****da pa***past** *da ... si***vod***nya* Мне надо попасть до ... сегодня
When shall I come back?	*Kag***da** *mnye vyer***noot***sa?* Когда мне вернуться

Train

- Permission is required to travel from one city to another in the Soviet Union, and your travel arrangements will almost certainly have been pre-booked. Owing to the long distances involved, inter-city travel is in sleeping cars (спальный вагон/*spal**niy** va**gon***), of which there are various categories: международный/*mizhdoona**rod**niy* are the most comfortable for very long journeys, in a 2-berth compartment with separate toilets; мягкий/***myakh**kee* is a luxury 4-berth compartment; купейный/*koo**pyei**niy* is a 4-berth compartment. Общий/***ob**shchee* and плацкартный/*plats**kart**niy* provide pre-booked seats in an ordinary compartment. Men and women share the same compartment, but men traditionally go out into the corridor when women are undressing.
- Carriages are comfortable with large windows and piped-in radio. When you enter a train, the проводник/*pravad**neek*** takes your ticket. He or she sits at the end of the corridor during the journey, and will automatically provide cups of tea (for a few kopecks) and wake you up at specified times.
- Most trains include dining-cars and buffets, but for long journeys it is advisable to take some food and drink with you.
- At the station (вокзал/*vak**zal***) timetables are divided into main and suburban lines, and use the 24-hour clock (always on Moscow time). Most main-line trains have a number. For journeys to the suburbs there are automatic ticket dispensers (smaller stations may have a booking office). Stations are zoned, and when the correct zone has been located, the right money should be inserted into the machine.
- It is possible to find porters to carry your luggage, and they will generally charge for each separate item.

How much is a ticket to ...?	***Skol**ka **stoy**eet beel**yet** f ...?* Сколько стоит билет в ...?
A ticket/two tickets to ...	***Adeen** beel**yet**/dva beel**yet**a da ...* Один билет/два билета до ...

Give me ...	***Da**eetye mnye ...* Дайте мне ...
... a single ticket	*... beel**yet** fa**deen** kan**yets*** билет в один конец
... a return ticket	*... beel**yet** too**da** ee a**brat**na* билет туда и обратно

I booked ...	*Ya zaka**zal*** **(man)**/*zaka**zala*** **(woman)** ... Я заказал/заказала ...
... an upper/lower berth	*... **verkh**nyeye/**neezh**nyeye **myes**ta* верхнее/нижнее место
... in a 4-berth sleeper	*... f koo**pyei**nam va**gon**ye* в купейном вагоне
... in a first-class 4-berth sleeper	*... f **myakh**kam va**gon**ye* в мягком вагоне
... in a first-class 2-berth sleeper	*... f mizhdoona**rod**nam va**gon**ye* в международном вагоне

When does ... leave for ...?	*Kag**da** at**khod**eet ... na ...?* Когда отходит ... на ...?
... the first train/next train/ last train	*... **pyer**viy/**slyed**ooyooshchee/ pas**lyed**nee **poy**ezd* первый/следующий/ последний поезд
From which platform?	*S ka**koy** plat**for**miy?* С какой платформы?

What time does the train arrive in ...?	*F katoram chasoo poyezd preebiyvayet f ...?* В котором часу поезд прибывает в ...?
How long does it take?	*Skolka vryeminee zaeemyot payezdka?* Сколько времени займёт поездка?
Is it direct, or do I have to change?	*Eta pryamoy poyezd, eelee boodyet pirisatka?* Это прямой поезд, или будет пересадка?
Where is the train timetable?	*Gdye raspeesaneeye payezdof?* Где расписание поездов?
When does train no. 5 leave?	*Kagda atpravlyayetsa poyezd nomir pyat?* Когда отправляется поезд номер пять?
What train is this?	*Kakoy etat poyezd?* Какой этот поезд?
Does it stop at ...?	*On astanavleevayetsa f ...?* Он останавливается в ...?
Is this seat taken?	*Eta myesta svabodna?* Это место свободно?
Can I put my case here?	*Mozhna pastaveet chemadan syooda?* Можно поставить чемодан сюда?
Can I open the window/ close the door?	*Mozhna atkriyt akno/zakriyt dvyer?* Можно открыть окно/ закрыть дверь?
Can I turn off the radio/ turn on the light	*Mozhna viyklyoocheet radeeo/fklyoocheet svyet?* Можно выключить радио/ включить свет?
Is smoking allowed?	*Kooreet zdyes razrishayetsa?* Курить здесь разрешается?

Where is ...?	*Gdye zdyes ...?* Где здесь ...?
... the buffet	*... boof**yet*** буфет
... the dining-car	*... va**gon**-rista**ran*** вагон-ресторан
... the smoking car	*... va**gon** dlya koor**yash**cheekh* вагон для курящих
... the sleeping car	*... **spal**niy va**gon*** спальный вагон
... the toilet	*... twal**yet*** туалет
Can you wake me at ... o'clock?	*Viy **mozh**itye razboo**deet** minya f ... chasof?* Вы можете разбудить меня в ... часов?
Bring me ...	*Preeni**seet**ye mnye ...* Принесите мне ...
... a glass of tea	*... sta**kan cha**ya* стакан чая
... another blanket	*... yish**cho** ade**ya**la* ещё одеяло
... a pillow	*... pa**doosh**koo* подушку
How long is the train stopping here?	***Skol**ka **vryem**inee **poy**ezd **bood**yet **stoy**eet zdyes?* Сколько времени поезд будет стоить здесь?
Can I get out?	***Mozh**na **viy**eetee?* Можно выйти?
How late is the train?	*Nas**kol**ka **poy**ezd apaz**dal**?* Насколько поезд опоздал?

You may see:

ПРИГОРОДНЫЕ ПОЕЗДА ***Pree**garadniye payez**da***	**Main-line trains**
ПОЕЗДА ДАЛЬНЕГО СЛЕДОВАНИЯ *Payez**da dal**nyeva slida**van**eeya*	**Suburban trains**
ПРИБЫТИЕ *Pree**biyt**eeye*	**Arrivals**
ОТПРАВЛЕНИЕ *Atprav**lyen**eeye*	**Departures**
НА МОСКВУ	**To Moscow**
НА ЛЕНИНГРАД	**To Leningrad**
К ТАКСИ	**Taxis**
СПРАВКИ ***Spraf**kee*	**Information**
ЗАЛ ОЖИДАНИЯ *Zal azhee**dan**eeya*	**Waiting room**
КАМЕРА ХРАНЕНИЯ БАГАЖА ***Kam**ira khran**yen**eeya ba**gazh**a*	**Left luggage office**
БЮРО НАХОДОК *Byoo**ro** na**khod**ak*	**Lost property**
ПЛАТФОРМА/ ПЕРРОН *Plat**form**a/Per**ron***	**Platform**
ПУТЬ *Poot*	**Line/Track**
Поезд номер ... ***Poy**ezd **nom**ir*	**Train number ...**
Вагон номер ... ***Vagon nom**ir*	**Coach number ...**
Место номер ... ***Myes**ta **nom**ir*	**Seat number ...**

Porter, take my luggage to the taxi	*Naseelshcheek, vazmeetye moy bagazh k taksee* Носильщик, возьмите мой багаж к такси

Air

- Any problems to do with air travel should be addressed to the Aeroflot Intourist desk (касса Аэрофлота/*kassa Aeraflota*) at the airport (аэропорт/*aeraport*) – there will be someone here who speaks English. Check-in time is usually about $1\frac{1}{2}$ hours before departure. Many airports are some way outside the town, with transfer by coach from the city terminal (аэровокзал/*aeravakzal*). Air transport is very popular in the Soviet Union for internal flights owing to the vast distances between towns, and in Moscow there are four separate airports. Though the procedure is relatively organised and queues at airports are not as bad as in the past, it is always advisable to leave plenty of time in case of delays.
- Departure lounges usually contain a buffet where drinks and sandwiches can be bought, along with a duty-free shop selling souvenirs and the same goods as can be obtained in Beriozka shops (see page 111).
- Listen out for the word посадка/*pasatka* (boarding), and also выход/*viykhat* (departure gate) along with the relevant number.
- Note that there is no separate non-smoking area on Soviet aeroplanes.

How do I get to the airport?	*Kak mnye dayekhat da aeraporta?* Как мне доехать до аэропорта?
Where is the booking office?	*Gdye beelyetniye kassiy?* Где билетные кассы?
What time is check-in?	*F katoram chasoo boodyet rigistratseeya?* В котором часу будет регистрация?

I would like ...	*Ya khat**yel** biy* (**man**)/ *Ya khat**yela** biy* (**woman**) Я хотел бы/Я хотела бы ...
... to book a ticket/ two tickets	... *zaka**zat** beel**yet**/dva beel**yet**a* заказать билет/два билета
... to Kiev/Riga/Tashkent	... *f **Kee**-ef/**Ree**goo/Tash**kent*** в Киев/Ригу/Ташкент
... a window seat	... ***myes**ta oo ak**na*** место у окна
... an aisle seat	... ***myes**ta oo pree**khoda*** место у прихода
... to change this reservation	... *pirines**tee** **e**tat za**kaz*** перенести этот заказ
... to cancel a reservation	... *annoo**leer**avat za**kaz*** аннулировать заказ

When is the next flight to ...?	*Kag**da** **slyed**ooyooshchee ryeis na ...?* Когда следующий рейс на ...?

Here is ...	*Vot ...* Вот ...
... my ticket/my luggage	... *moy beel**yet**/moy ba**gazh*** мой билет/мой багаж
... my hand luggage/my visa	... *moy rooch**noy** ba**gazh**/ma**ya** **vee**za* мой ручной багаж/моя виза
... my passport/my customs declaration	... *moy **pas**part/ma**ya** dikla**rat**seeya* мой паспорт/моя декларация

Excuse me, I can't find my seat	*Prasteetye, ya ni magoo naeetee mayo myesta* Простите, я не могу найти моё место
Stewardess! I feel sick	*Styooardyessa! Minya tashneet* Стюардесса! Меня тошнит
Bring me a newspaper/ a pillow/some water	*Preeniseetye mnye zhoornal/ padooshkoo/vadiy* Принесите мне журнал/ подушку/воды

You may see:

РЕГИСТРАЦИЯ БАГАЖА *Rigeestratseeya bagazha*	**Luggage check-in**
ВЫХОД НА ПОСАДКУ *Viykhat na pasatkoo*	**Departure gate**
ПОСАДКА *Pasatka*	**Boarding/Transit**
ВЫДАЧА БАГАЖА *Viydacha bagazha*	**Luggage collection point**
ЗАСТЕГНУТЬ РЕМНИ *Zastyegnoot ryemnee*	**Fasten seat belts**
НЕ КУРИТЬ *Ni kooreet*	**No smoking**
ЗАПАСНОЙ ВЫХОД *Zapasnoy viykhat*	**Emergency exit**

You may hear:

Abivlyaetsa pasatka na samalyot Обьявляется посадка на самолёт	**Boarding is announced**
Viylyet zadirzheevayetsa Вылет задерживается	**The flight has been delayed**

SHOPPING

- Visitors to the Soviet Union should not expect to find shops full of well-stocked shelves, and any items regarded as essential, such as cosmetics, toiletries, soap, toothpaste, medicines, holiday first-aid kit, batteries, photographic supplies, tights, books and magazines should be brought from home. Visitors from the West are also advised to bring a plug with them – hotel basins do not always provide them. Everyday goods such as toilet paper or sugar are also difficult to find at various times.
- Foreign tourists are generally guided to the hard-currency (Берёзка/*Beriozka*) shops, where goods can be bought more cheaply than elsewhere, but must be paid for in sterling, dollars, etc. These shops stock imported goods, souvenirs, duty-free drink, cameras, watches, jewellery, etc. and items that are not available to the general public such as perfume, coffee and wine. Credit cards can also be used for

purchases in Beriozka shops, but be sure to ascertain the exchange rate before you agree to use this method of payment (ask *K**a**koy koors abm**ye**na*/Какой курс обмена?). Although credit cards are increasingly accepted in shops and restaurants in the Soviet Union, you may find that a different set of prices operates, and you can end up paying three times the cash price. If you are on the lookout for something unusual to bring home, such as an antique samovar or picture, the place to go is a second-hand shop (комиссионный магазин/*kameesee**yon**niy magaz**een***). Note, however, that it is illegal to buy goods from private individuals.

- For anything else, it is probably easiest to find what you want in a large department store, such as ГУМ (*GUM*) in Moscow or Гостиный Двор (*Gas**tee**niy Dvor*) in Leningrad. Stores are very crowded, particularly at weekends, but it is worth persevering. Opening times vary, but most shops are open from 9 am to 7 pm from Monday to Saturday.
- The names of shops often begin with Дом/*Dom* (House), e.g. Дом Обуви/*Dom **O**boovee* – the House of Footwear, i.e. shoe shop.
- Food can be bought in a food store, shop or supermarket, or at the food counter in a department store. Small shops generally bear the name of the product, along with a picture of it, e.g. мясо/***mya**sa* (meat), рыба/***ri**yba* (fish), молоко/*mala**ko*** (milk).
- Food shops are open seven days a week, from early in the morning until 7 pm, with a break for lunch between 1 and 2 pm. As shops are state owned, they all sell the same goods at the same price. Fresh food is often in short supply and limited to whatever is in season, and there may be long queues to buy such things as meat. For fruit and vegetables, many people prefer to shop in the market, where private produce is sold. Though often exorbitant in price, the quality tends to be better, and you may be able to bargain. Markets open very early in the morning, and are especially busy at weekends and before public holidays.

Where's the nearest ...?	*Gdye na**khod**eetsa blee**zha**eeshee ...?* Где находится ближайший ...?
... food store	*... gastra**nom*** гастроном
... department store	*... ooneever**mak*** универмаг
... food shop	*... **prod**mak* продмаг
... market	*... **riy**nak* рынок
... supermarket	*... ooneever**sam*** универсам
Do you know where ... shop is?	*Viy ni **zna**yetye gdye zdyes ... maga**zeen**?* Вы не знаете где здесь ... магазин?
When does it open/close?	*Kag**da** on atkriy**va**yetsa/ zakriy**va**yetsa?* Когда он открывается/ закрывается?
Is it open on Sunday?	*On ra**bot**ayet f vaskri**syen**ye?* Он работает в воскресенье?
Where can I buy?	*Gdye **mozh**na koo**peet** ...?* Где можно купить ...?
... souvenirs	*... soovi**neer**iy* сувениры
... books/records	*... **knee**gee/plas**teen**kee* книги/пластинки
... clothes/something to eat	*... **adyezh**diy/**shto**-neeboot pa**koo**shat* одежды/что-нибудь покушать

How do I get there?	*Kak praee**tee** too**da**?* Как пройти туда?

Paying for the goods

- Although some stores and food supermarkets are now self-service, in most you have to queue for the goods and then queue again to pay. The assistant in the first queue may give you a ticket quoting the name of the item, name or number of the department and the price; if not, you will have to give this information to the cashier yourself. Having paid, you will be given a receipt (чек/*chek*) which authorises you to collect your purchase. In some stores, this takes place at a central collection point, signposted выдача покупок/***viy**dacha pa**koop**ak* or контроль/*kan**trol***.
- See also **Shopping in a department store** on page 107.

I'll take it. How much is that?	*Ya bye**roo** eta. **Skol**ka smin**ya**?* Я беру это. Сколько с меня?
Please write it down	*Napee**sheet**ye, pa**zhal**asta* Напишите, пожалуйста
Write me out a bill, please	*Pa**zhal**asta, **viy**peesheetye chek* Пожалуйста, выпишите чек
Where do I pay?	*Gdye **na**da pla**teet**?* Где надо платить?
Where's the cash desk?	*Gdye **kas**sa?* Где касса?
Do you take pounds/dollars/roubles?	*Viy bir**yot**ye **foon**tiy/**doll**ariy/roob**lee**?* Вы берёте фунты/доллары/рубли?
Can I pay by credit card?	***Mozh**na pla**teet** kri**deet**noy **kart**achkoy?* Можно платить кредитной карточкой?

You may hear:

*Plateetye **fkassoo** … rooblyei* Платите в кассу … рублей	**Pay at the cash desk … roubles**
Kooda/Kakoy atdyel? Куда/Какой одтел?	**Where/which department is that from?**
Vash chek, pazhalasta Ваш чек, пожалуйста	**Your bill, please**
Vot vam kveetantseeya/sdacha Вот вам квитанция/сдача	**Here's your receipt/change**

You may see:

КАССА *Kassa*	**Cash desk**
ВЫДАЧА ПОКУПОК *Viydacha pakoopak*	**Collection point for purchases**

Shopping for food

Some common food shops

baker's	*boolachnaya* БУЛОЧНАЯ
cake shop	*kandeetyerskaya* КОНДИТЕРСКАЯ
dairy products	*malochnaya/malako* МОЛОЧНАЯ/МОЛОКО
fish	*riyba* РЫБА
fruit and vegetables	*ovashchee-frooktiy* ОВОЩИ-ФРУКТЫ
juice and mineral water	*sokee-vadiy* СОКИ-ВОДЫ

grocer's	*bakal**ye**ya* БАКАЛЕЯ
meat and poultry	***mya**sa-**pteet**sa* МЯСО-ПТИЦА

Bread and cake shops

- Most bread shops are self-service, and sell a variety of black and white bread and rolls. Black bread is popular in the Soviet Union, and there are many different types. Bread and cake shops are often combined, and also sell sweets, chocolate, tea and coffee.

Give me ..., please	***Da**eetye mnye, paz**hal**asta ...* Дайте мне, пожалуйста ...
... a loaf of brown/white bread	*... **chor**niy/**byel**iy khlyep* чёрный/белый хлеб
... a large loaf/French stick	*... boo**khan**koo/ba**ton*** буханку/батон
... a cake/two rolls	*... pee**rozh**naye/dvye **bool**achkee* пирожное/две булочки
... a fruit tart/a pie	*... tort s**frook**tamee/pee**rok*** торт с фруктами/пирог
... a packet of biscuits/coffee/tea	*... **pach**koo pi**chen**ya/**kof**ye/**cha**ya* пачку печенья/кофе/чая
... a packet/box/half a kilo of sweets	*... ka**rop**koo/**pach**koo/palkee**lo** kan**fyet*** коробку/пачку/полкило конфет
... of chocolates	*... shaka**lat**niykh kan**fyet*** шоколадных конфет
... a bar of chocolate	*... **pleet**koo shaka**lad**a* плитку шоколада

Milk and dairy products

- Milk and dairy products are very popular in the Soviet Union, and are sold in packets, cartons or bottles with different coloured tops. Сметана/*smetana*, or sour cream, is a common accompaniment to all kinds of dishes from pancakes to soups and stews. Кефир/*Kefeer* is a popular drink rather like buttermilk, and ряженка/*ryazhenka*, a sour, baked milk, is similar. The nearest thing to yoghurt is простокваша/*prastakvasha*. Various types of cottage or curd cheese and yoghurt can also be bought fresh from the market.

I'd like ...	*Ya khatyel* (**man**)/*khatyela* (**woman**) *biy ...* Я хотел/хотела бы ...
... a bottle of milk	*... bootiylkoo malaka* бутылку молока
... a packet of curd cheese/ yoghurt	*... pakyet tvoraga/ prastakvashee* пакет творога/ простокваши
... a carton of sour cream/ cream	*... pachkoo smetaniy/sleevak* пачку сметаны/сливок
... 100 grams of butter/ 200 grams of cheese	*... sto gramm masla/dvyestee gramm siyra* сто грамм масла/ двести грамм сыра
Five/ten eggs, please	*Pyat/Dyesyat yaits, pazhalasta* Пять/Десять яиц, пожалуйста
Have you any ...?	*Oo vas yist ...?* У вас есть ...?
... sheep's cheese	*... briynza* брынза

... mayonnaise	*... maya**nez*** майонез
... ice cream	*... ma**rozh**enaye* мороженое

Groceries

Do you have any ...?	*Oo vas yist ...?* У вас есть ...?
... honey/jam	*... myot/var**yen**ye* мёд/варенье
... margarine	*... marga**reen*** маргарин
... lard/oil	*... zheer/ras**teet**ilnoye **mas**la* жир/растительное масло
... raisins	*... eez**yoom*** изюм
... tinned meat/fish	*... **myas**niye/**riyb**niye kan**syer**viy* мясные/рыбные консервы

Give me ..., please	***Da**eetye mnye, pa**zhal**asta ...* Дайте мне, пожалуйста ...
... a packet of sugar	*... **pach**koo **sakh**aroo* пачку сахару
... granulated/lump	*... **sakh**arniy **pye**sak/**sakh**ar-rafee**nat*** сахарный песок/сахар-рафинад
... a jar of salted cucumbers	*... **ban**koo sal**yon**iykh agoort**sof*** банку солёных огурцов
... of pickled mushrooms	*... maree**nov**anniykh greep* маринованных гриб
... of peas	*... **gor**akha* гороха

What fruit juices do you have?
*Ka**kee**ye frook**to**viye **so**kee oo vas yist?*
Какие фруктовые соки у вас есть?

Fruit and vegetables

I'll have a kilo/$1\frac{1}{2}$ kilos/ 2 kilos/3 kilos …
***Da**eetye kee**lo**/palta**ra** kee**lo**/ dva kee**lo**/tree kee**lo** …*
Дайте кило/полтора кило/два кило/три кило …

… of onions
*… **loo**ka*
лука

… of carrots
*… mar**ko**vee*
моркови

How much is $\frac{1}{2}$ kilo/ a kilo …?
***Skol**ka s**to**yeet palkee**lo**/ kee**lo**… ?*
Сколько стоит полкило/ кило …?

… of tomatoes/cucumber
*… pamee**dor**af/agoort**sof***
помидоров/орурцов

… of lettuce/radishes/ mushrooms
*… sa**la**ta/ri**dees**kee/**gree**baf*
салата/редиски/грибов

I'll have …
*Ya vaz**moo** …*
Я возьму …

… a cabbage
*… ka**poos**too*
капусту

… a cauliflower
*… tsvyet**noo**yoo ka**poos**too*
цветную капусту

… a green pepper
*… **pyer**its*
перец

… some garlic
*… chis**nok***
чеснок

… black olives/nuts
*… mas**lee**niy/ar**yekh**ee*
маслины/орехи

Half a kilo/a kilo/ two kilos ... please	*Palkee**lo**/kee**lo**/dva kee**lo** ..., pa**zhal**asta* Полкило/кило/два кило ... пожалуйста
... of apples/pears/apricots	*... **yab**lak/groosh/abree**kos**af* яблок/груш/абрикосов
... of oranges/peaches/ plums	*... apyel**seen**af/**pyer**seekaf/ sleef* апельсинов/персиков/ слив
... of strawberries/raspberries/ cherries	*... **kloob**neekee/ma**lee**niy/ **vee**shen* клубинки/малины/ вишен
... of lemons/tangerines/ figs	*... lee**mon**af/manda**reen**af/ een**zheer**a* лимонов/мандаринов/ инжира
Give me ...	***Da**eetye mnye ...* Дайте мне ...
... a pineapple/a grapefruit	*... ana**nas**/**gryeip**froot* ананас/грейпфрут
... a melon/water melon	*... **diyn**yoo/ar**booz*** дыню/арбуз
... sour cherries/bananas/ dates	*... cher**yesh**nee/ba**na**niy/ **fee**neekee* черешни/бананы/ финики
... a bunch of grapes	*... vina**grat*** виноград
Can I try one?	***Mozh**na pa**pro**bavat?* Можно попробовать?
How much does that come to altogether?	***Skol**ka eta **stoy**eet fsyo **fmyes**tye?* Сколько это стоит всё вместе?

Shopping in department stores

Where's the ladies/gents/ children's clothes department?

*Gdye at**dyel** '**zhen**skaya/ moozh**ska**ya/**dyet**skaya ad**yezh**da'?*
Где отдел "женская/ мужская/детская одежда"?

• Look out for the following departments:

ПОДАРКИ *pa**dar**kee*	**Gifts**	КНИГИ ***knee**gee*	**Books**
СУВЕНИРЫ *soovi**neer**iy*	**Souvenirs**	ГРАМПЛАС-ТИНКИ *gramplas**teen**kee*	**Records**
МЕХА ***mye**kha*	**Furs**	ФАРФОР ***far**far*	**China**
ДУХИ *doo**khee***	**Perfumes**	КУХОННАЯ ПОСУДА *koo**khon**naya pa**soo**da*	**Kitchenware**
ОБУВЬ ***o**boof*	**Footwear**	МЕБЕЛЬ ***mye**byel*	**Furniture**
ГОЛОВНЫЕ УБОРЫ *galav**ni**ye oo**bo**riy*	**Hats**	КОЖГАЛАН-ТЕРЕЯ *kozhgalantir**ye**ya*	**Leather goods**
ТКАНИ ***tka**nee*	**Fabrics**	ЧАСЫ *cha**siy***	**Watches**
ИГРУШКИ *ee**groosh**kee*	**Toys**		

Shopping for clothes

I'm just looking

*Ya **pros**ta smat**ryoo***
Я просто смотрю

Show me ... please

*Poka**zheet**ye, pa**zhal**asta, ...*
Покажите, пожалуйста, ...

... that (over there)

... vot eta
вот это

... that skirt/blouse/shirt	*... too* ***yoop****koo/****blooz****koo/ roo****bash****koo* ту юбку/блузку/рубашку
... in the window	*... na vee****treen****ye* на витрине

How much are ...?	***Skol****ka* ***stoy****at ...?* Сколько стоят ...?
How much is ...?	***Skol****ka* ***stoy****eet ...?* Сколько стоит ...?
I like ... very much	*Mnye* ***och****in* ***nra****veetsa ...* Мне очень нравится ...

- See the Wordlist (page 145) for individual items of clothing.

Colours

black	***chor****niy* чёрный	**yellow**	***zhol****tiy* жёлтый
white	***bye****liy* белый	**brown**	*ka****reech****nyeviy* коричневый
red	***kras****niy* красный	**grey**	***sye****riy* серый
light blue	*galoo****boy*** голубой	**orange**	*a****ran****zheviy* оранжевый
dark blue	*seenee* синий	**pink**	***ro****zaviy* розовый
green	*zil****yon****iy* зелёный	**purple**	*poor****poor****niy* пурпурный

What size is it?	*Ka****koy*** *raz****myer****?* Какой размер?
Can I try it on?	***Mozh****na pree****myer****eet?* Можно примерить?
Is there a mirror here?	*Zdyes* ***zyer****kala?* Здесь зеркало?
What do you think?	*Shto viy* ***doo****mayete?* Что вы думаете?

It doesn't suit me	*Mnye **e**ta ni pad**khod**eet* Мне это не подходит
It's too small/big for me	***E**ta mnye **sleesh**kam **ma**la/vyelee**ko*** Это мне слишком мало/велико
It's too short/long/tight	***E**ta **sleesh**kam **kor**atka/ **dleen**na/**tyes**na* Это слишком коротко/ длинно/тесно
The shoes are too wide/narrow	***Toof**lee **sleesh**kam sheera**kee**/ **ooz**kee* Туфли слишком широки/ узки
I don't like the colour	*Tsvyet mnye ni **nra**veetsa* Цвет мне не нравится
Do you have it in another ...	*Oo vas yist to zhe droo**go**va ...* У вас есть то же другого ...
... size/colour/style?	*... raz**myer**a/**tsvyet**a/fa**son**a?* размера/цвета/фасона?

Materials

cotton	хлопок ***khlo**pak*	**velvet**	бархат ***bar**khat*
wool	шерсть *shairst*	**linen**	полотно *palat**no***
nylon	нейлон *nyei**lon***	**lace**	кружево ***krooz**heva*
silk	шёлк *sholk*	**leather**	кожа ***ko**zha*

Have you got anything ...?	*Oo vas yist **shto**-neeboot ...?* У вас есть что-нибудь ...?
... smaller/bigger	*... pa**myen**shye/pa**bol**shye* поменьше/побольше
... cheaper/better	*... padi**shev**lye/pada**rozh**ye* подешевле/подороже

Can I change this?	***Mozh**na abmin**yat** eta?* Можно обменять это?
I'll take it	*Ya vaz**moo** eta* Я возьму это
Please can you wrap it up	*Zavyer**neet**ye, pazh**al**asta* Заверните, пожалуйста

Shopping for books, stationery and records

- Books are very cheap in the Soviet Union but the range is limited. Reading is extremely popular and whole editions sell out within hours of reaching the shops. Second-hand books can be bought at a Букинистический магазин/*Bookeenee-**stee**cheskee maga**zeen***, and sometimes at second-hand shops, which also sell pictures, silver, old samovars, etc. It is advisable to check that you are allowed to take anything bought in one of these shops out of the country, and to get a receipt for it.
- Stationery shops carry the usual range of writing paper, pens, pencils, etc. Newspapers and magazines can be bought from news-stands and kiosks and in Underground stations, along with maps, guide-books, postcards, envelopes and stamps. Hotel kiosks generally stock a few foreign newspapers such as *The Times* and the *New York Herald Tribune.*

Have you got an English–Russian dictionary	*Oo vas yist angla–**roos**kee sla**var*** У вас есть англо–русский словарь
Where's the newspaper kiosk?	*Gdye gaz**yet**niy kee**osk**?* Где газетный киоск?
Do you have ...?	*Oo vas yist ...?* У вас есть ...?
... an English newspaper	*... an**glees**kaya gaz**yet**a* английская газета

... an American magazine	... *amiree**kan**skee zhoor**nal*** американский журнал
... a map of the city	... ***kar**ta **gor**ada* карта города
... a plan of the metro	... *plan mi**tro*** план метро
... a guidebook	... *pootiva**deet**yel* путеводитель
... postcards	... *at**kriy**tkee* открытки
... envelopes	... *kanv**yer**tiy* конверты
... paper	... *boo**ma**ga* бумага

- Records are extremely good value, and if you can work out what you want, you can pick up, among other things, excellent classical recordings. In record shops such as Мелодия/*Me**lod**iya* in Moscow you can listen to them first. A board tells you what recordings are in stock, and you quote the number of the recording you want to the assistant.

Can I listen to it?	***Mozh**na pas**loo**shat?* Можно послушать?

Shopping for souvenirs

- The Берёзка/*Be**rioz**ka* shops stock all the traditional Russian crafts and souvenirs, such as amber jewellery and ornaments, soapstone boxes and animals, bone and ivory carvings, headscarves, nests of dolls, fur hats and coloured shawls. Other gifts to take home are the red, black and gold Khokhloma bowls, spoons and trays, and rather more expensive Palekh-ware lacquered papier-mache boxes. These shops also sell different brands of vodka (водка/***vot**ka*) and wine (вино/*vee**no***) and tins of caviar (икра/*ee**kra***). Souvenirs can also be found in department stores and many toy shops. Beriozka shops of varying sizes can be found in Intourist hotels, and hotel kiosks also stock a limited range of the same goods.

How much is ...?	***Skol**ka **stoy**eet?* Сколько стоит ...?
... the spoon/tablecloth/ nest of dolls	*... **lozh**ka/skat**yert**/mat**ryosh**ka* ложка/скатерть/ матрёшка
... the shawl/head square	*... shal/pla**tok*** шаль/платок
... fur hat/hat with earflaps	*... **myekh**avaya **shap**ka/oo**shan**ka* меховая шапка/ушанка
I want to buy ...	*Ya kha**choo** koo**peet** ...* Я хочу купить ...
... a Palekh box	*... **pal**ikhskooyoo shka**tool**koo* палехскую шкатулку
... an amber brooch/amber beads	*... yan**tar**nooyoo **brosh**koo/ yan**tar**niye **boo**siy* янтарную брошку/ янтарные бусы
... this ring/necklace	*... eta kal**tso**/azhir**yel**ye* это кольцо/ожерелье
... a camera/a watch	*... fata-appa**rat**/cha**siy*** фото-аппарат/часы

Other gift items

amber	*yan**tar*** янтарь
ceramics, pottery	*ki**ra**meeka* керамика
(gold) chain	*(zala**ta**ya) tsi**poch**ka* (золотая) цепочка
doll	***kook**la* кукла

SERVICES

Bank

- Banks are open from approximately 9.30 am to 12.30 pm from Monday to Friday, but for the purposes of changing money, it is generally easier to go to the currency exchange office at the hotel or airport, where hours are longer. See **Currency Exchange** on page 15.

Where's the nearest bank?
*Gdye bleez**ha**eeshee bank?*
Где ближайший банк?

Can I cash a cheque?
***Mozh**na paloo**cheet dyen**gee pa **chek**oo?*
Можно получить деньги по чеку?

Post Office

- Main post offices have different counters for such things as buying stamps, postcards and envelopes (with or without stamps attached), sending parcels, registered letters, etc. Stamps are 5 kopecks for internal mail, 50 kopecks for all other countries. When sending a packet or small parcel abroad, the assistant will weigh the contents unwrapped. You should then ask him to wrap it up (*Zavir**neet**ye*/ Заверните), and he will hand it over for you to write your name and address on the back. You will then be given a receipt for the transaction.
- Post boxes, found at post offices and on the walls of buildings, are red for local mail, blue for all other mail.
- Most post offices have telegraph (телеграф/*tili**graf***) and telephone (телефон/*tili**fon***) sections. To send a telegram home, ask for an international telegram form or pick one up from the counter.

Where is the nearest post office? — *Gdye blee**zha**eeshaya **poch**ta?*
Где ближайшая почта?

How much is ...? — ***Skol**ka **stoy**eet ...?*
Сколько стоит ...?

... a letter to England — *... pees**mo** f **An**glee'ee*
письмо в Англии

... to America — *... f Sayedeen**yon**niye **Shta**tiy*
в Соединённые Штаты

... a postcard to Canada — *... at**kriyt**ka f Ka**na**doo*
открытка в Канаду

... to Australia — *... f Af**stra**leeyoo*
в Австарлию

A stamp at 50 kopecks, please — ***Mar**ka za pitdis**yat** kap**ye**yek, pa**zhal**asta*
Марка за пятьдесят копеек, пожалуйста

Two stamps/five stamps at 70	*Dvye **mar**kee/pyat **mar**ak za simdisyat* Две марки/пять марок за семьдесят
I want to send ...	*Ya kha**choo** pas**lat** ...* Я хочу послать ...
... a packet	*... bandi**rol*** бандероль
... a registered packet	*... zakaz**noo**yoo bandi**rol*** заказную бандероль
... a parcel	*... pa**siyl**koo* посылку
... an insured parcel	*... **tsyen**nooyoo pa**siyl**koo* ценную посылку
... a telegram (international)	*... tili**gram**moo (mizhdoona**rod**nooyoo)* телеграмму (международную)
... an airmail letter	*... aveea-pees**mo*** авиаписьмо
... a registered letter	*... zakaz**noye** pees**mo*** заказное письмо

Please give me ...	***Da**eetye pa**zhal**asta ...* Дайте пожалуйста ...
... a postcard	*... at**kriyt**koo* отркрытку
... an airmail envelope	*... aveea-kan**vyert*** авиаконверт
... a stamped envelope	*... kan**vyert** s**mar**koy* конверт с маркой
... a form	*... blank* бланк
... a telegram form	*... blank tili**gram**miy* бланк телеграммы

Where is . . .?	*Gdye . . .?* Где . . .?
. . . the post box	*. . . pach**to**viy **yash**cheek* почтовый ящик
. . . the poste restante counter	*. . . ak**no** da vas**tryeb**avaneeya* окно до востребования
. . . counter 7	*. . . ak**no** syem* окно семь
Do you have a letter/money order for me?	*Oo vas yist pees**mo**/piri**vot** dlya min**ya**?* У вас есть письмо/перевод для меня?

You may hear:

*Vam **na**da za**pol**neet blank* Вам надо заполнить бланк	**You have to fill in a form**
*Raspee**sheet**yes* Распишитесь	**Sign here**

You may see:

МАРКИ ***Mar**kee*	**Stamps**
ПРОДАЖА КОНВЕРТОВ, ОТКРЫТОК *Pra**da**zha kan**vyer**taf, at**kriy**tak*	**Envelopes, postcards**
ПРИЁМ И ВЫДАЧА ПОСЫЛОК *Pree**yom** ee **viy**dacha pas**iy**lak*	**Parcels**
ПРИЁМ И ВЫДАЧА ПЕРЕВОДОВ *Pree**yom** ee **viy**dacha piri**vo**daf*	**Money orders**

Telephone

- Local calls are very cheap, and there are plenty of phone boxes (телефон-автомат/*tili**fon**-afta**mat***) on the street. They can also be made free of charge from hotel rooms. When answering the phone, Russians generally just say 'Hello' (*A**llo***/Алло or ***Sloo**shayoo*/Слушаю) rather than giving a name or number.
- Long-distance calls can be made from an international telephone point (международный телефонный переговорный пункт/ *mizhdoona**rod**niy tili**fon**niy piriga**vor**niy poonkt*) at a main post office, or from the hotel. In either case, calls should be booked in advance. You will be required to give the name of the country, the number and to say when you want to be put through, and for how many minutes. You may also be asked the name of the person you want to speak to. In a post office, wait until you hear a loudspeaker announcement telling you which number booth (кабина/*ka**bee**na*) to go in. If you have arranged to make the call through your hotel, be prepared to wait by the phone. You will be advised when your time is nearly up, and asked if you want to extend the call.

Emergency numbers:	**Fire**	**01**	**Police**	**02**
	Ambulance	**03**	**Gas**	**04**

Can I telephone from here?	***Mozh**na at vas pazva**neet**?* Можно от вас позвонить?
Can you show me how to phone?	*Paka**zheet**ye mnye, kak pazva**neet*** Покажите мне, как позвонить
I need this number	*Mnye **noozh**en etat **nom**ir* Мне нужен этот номер

Extension no. 9	*Da**ba**vachniy **nom**ir **dyev**yat* Добавочный номер девять
Can I speak to Tanya?	*Paza**veet**ye **Tan**yoo* Позовите Таню
Can you repeat that?	*Paft**areet**ye, pa**zhal**asta* Повторите, пожалуйста
Speak slowly	*Gav**areet**ye **myed**linna* Говорите медленно
When will she/he be in?	*Kag**da** a**na**/on **bood**yet?* Когда она/он будет?
It's … speaking	***E**ta gav**areet** …* Это говорит …
Say I'll ring back later	*Piri**da**eetye, shto ya pazvan**yoo** **po**zzhe* Передайте, что я позвоню позже

You may hear:

*Kto gav**areet**?* Кто говорит?	**Who's speaking?**
*Gav**areet**ye **grom**che* Говорите громче	**Can you speak up?**
*Padazh**deet**ye ad**noo** mee**noot**achkoo* Подождите одну минуточку	**Hold the line a moment**
*Ye**yo**/Ye**vo** nyet* Её/его нет	**She's/He's not in**
*A**na**/On **bood**yet **chyer**iz chas* Она/Он будет через час	**She'll/He'll be back in an hour**
***Mozh**na piri**dat**?* Можно передать?	**Can I take a message?**
*Viy a**sheeb**lees* Вы ошиблись	**You've got the wrong number**

International calls

Where's the nearest international telephone point?	*Gdye blee**zha**eeshee mizhdoona**rod**niy piriga**vor**niy poonkt?* Где ближайший международный переговорный пункт?
I want to book a call ...	*Ya kha**choo** zaka**zat** razga**vor** ...* Я хочу заказать разговор ...
... to England/America	*... s **An**gleeyoo/f Say**sha*** с Англию/в США
... for 10 o'clock	*... na **dyes**yat cha**sof*** на десять часов
... for 3 minutes/for 5 minutes	*... na tree mee**noo**tiy/na pyat mee**noot*** на три минуты/на пять минут

You may hear:

***Skol**ka mee**noot**?* Сколько минут?	**For how long?**
S kyem? С кем?	**Who do you want to speak to?**
***Zan**yata* Занято	**It's engaged**
*Ni kla**deet**ye **troop**koo* Не кладите трубку	**Don't hang up**
*Gava**reet**ye* Говорите	**Go ahead**
*Asta**las** **tol**ka ad**na** mee**noo**ta* Осталась только одна минута	**You've got just one minute left**
*Vas **pros**yat k tili**fon**oo* Вас просят к телефону	**You're wanted on the phone**

Hairdresser's

Where is the hairdresser's?	*Gdye zdyes pareek-**makh**irskaya?* Где здесь парикмахерская?
I want to make an appointment ...	*Ya kha**choo** zapee**sat**sa ...* Я хочу записаться ...
... for today/tomorrow/ Wednesday	*... na si**vod**nya/**zaf**tra/sri**doo*** на сегодня/завтра/ среду
Please ...	*Pa**zhal**asta ...* Пожалуйста ...
... cut my hair	*... padstree**geet**ye min**ya*** подстригите меня
... give me a trim	*... padravn**ya**eetye mnye **vol**asiy* подровняйте мне волосы
... wash and set my hair	*... **viy**moytye ee oola**zheet**ye mnye **vol**asiy* вымойте и уложите мне волосы
... give me a perm	*... **sdyel**ayetye mnye pirman**yent*** сделайте мне перманент
Can you colour/lighten my hair?	***Mozh**na pak**ra**seet/ abit**svyet**eet mnye **vol**asiy?* Можно покрасить/ обесцветить мне волосы?
I want it cut with scissors/ a razor	*Ya kha**choo** pad**streech**sa **nozh**neetsamee/**breet**voy* Я хочу подстричься ножницами/бритвой
Please blow dry it	*Oola**zheet**ye **fyen**am, pa**zhal**asta* Уложите феном, пожалуйста

The water/dryer is too hot/cold	*Vada/soosheelka sleeshkam garyacha/kholadna* Вода/сушилка слишком горяча/холодна
Not too short, please	*Ni sleeshkam koratka, pazhalasta* Не слишком коротко, пожалуйста
Give me a parting on this side/in the middle	*Sdyelayetye mnye prabor setoy staraniy/f sirideenye* Сделайте мне пробор с этой стороны/в середине
I don't want any hairspray	*Byez laka, pazhalasta* Без лака, пожалуйста
I'd like a shave	*Pabryeitye minya* Побрейте меня
Trim my moustache/beard	*Padstreegeetye mnye oosiy/boradoo* Подстригите мне усы/бороду
I don't want any hair oil	*Ni smaziyvayetye mnye volasiy* Не смазываете мне волосы
Please give me a manicure/face pack	*Sdyelayetye mnye maneekyoor/kasmitee-cheskooyoo maskoo, pazhalasta* Сделайте мне маникюр/косметическую маску, пожалуйста

Cleaning

Where's the nearest dry cleaner's?	*Gdye bleezhaeeshaya kheemcheestka?* Где ближайшая химчистка?

I want to put this in for fast cleaning

*Ya kha**choo** at**dat** eta f **sroch**nooyoo kheem**cheest**koo*
Я хочу отдать это в срочную химчистку

Please can you ...

*Viy **mozh**etye ... pa**zhal**asta?*
Вы можете ...
пожалуйста?

... clean this coat/this suit

*... pa**chees**teet eta pal**to**/etat kast**yoom***
почистить это пальто/
этот костюм

... press these trousers

*... at**par**eet etee **bryoo**kee*
отпарить эти брюки

... iron this dress

*... pa**gla**deet eta **plat**ye*
погладить это платье

Can this stain be removed?

***Mozh**na **viy**vistee eta pyit**no**?*
Можно вывести это пятно?

This hole needs mending

***Na**da za**shto**pat etoo **diyr**koo*
Надо заштопать эту дырку

When will it be ready?

*Kag**da** eta **bood**yet ga**to**va?*
Когда это будет готово?

Repairs

My watch is broken

*Cha**siy** **slo**maniy*
Часы сломаны

It's running fast/slow

***A**nee spi**shat**/atstayoot*
Они спешат/отстают

I need to get my camera repaired

*Mnye **noozh**na atriman**teer**avat fata-appa**rat***
Мне нужно
отремонтировать фото-
аппарат

The flash isn't working

***Fspiysh**ka ni fklyoo**cha**yetsa*
Вспышка не включается

The shutter doesn't work

*Ni ra**bo**tayet **viy**dirzhka*
Не работает выдержка

Can you mend it?	***Mozh**na eta pachee**neet**?* Можно это починить?
When will it be ready?	*Kag**da** eta **bood**yet ga**to**va?* Когда это будет готово?

Please ...	*Pa**zhal**asta ...* Пожалуйста ...

... sew on a button	*... pree**shei**tye **poo**gaveetsoo* пришейте пуговицу
... sew on a strap	*... pree**shei**tye rimi**shok*** пришейте ремешок
... change the zip	*... zami**neet**ye **mol**neeyoo* замените молнию

Can you patch/clean this?	***Mozh**na zala**tat**/pa**chees**teet eta?* Можно залатать/почистить это?
Please mend these shoes	*Pachee**neet**ye, pa**zhal**asta, etee **toof**lee* Почините, пожалуйста, эти туфли
Replace the heels/soles	*Paminy**a**eetye kab**loo**kee/pad**myot**kee* Поменяйте каблуки/подмётки

At the tobacco kiosk

- Russians are very strict about smoking, which is not allowed in theatres, cinemas, on public transport and in other public places. Look out for no smoking signs: У НАС НЕ КУРЯТ; КУРИТЬ ВОСПРЕЩАЕТСЯ; НЕ КУРИТЬ, etc.
- As well as filter-tipped cigarettes, many Russians like to smoke traditional Russian cigarettes (папиросы/*papee**ro**siy*), which are very strong and smoked through long paper tubes.

Do you know where there's a tobacco kiosk?	*Viy ni **zna**yetye, gdye zdyes ta**bach**niy kee**osk**?* Вы не знаете, где здесь табачный киоск?
Give me . . ., please	***Da**eetye mnye, pa**zhal**asta . . .* Дайте мне, пожалуйста . . .
. . . cigarettes	*. . . seegar**yet**iy* сигареты
. . . filter tip/non-filter tip	*. . . **sfeel**tram/byez **feel**tra* с фильтром/без фильтра
. . . Russian cigarettes	*. . . papee**ro**siy* папиросы
. . . cigars	*. . . see**gar**iy* сигары
. . . pipe tobacco	*. . . **troo**bachniy ta**bak*** трубочный табак
What brands have you got?	*Ka**kee**ye **mar**kee oo vas yest?* Какие марки у вас есть?
Do you have any English/ American cigarettes?	*Oo vas yest an**glees**keeye/ amiree**kan**skeeye seegar**yet**iy?* У вас есть английские/ американские сигареты?
A carton, please	*A**deen** blok, pa**zhal**asta* Один блок, пожалуйста
I want . . .	*Ya kha**choo** . . .* Я хочу . . .
. . . some matches	*. . . **speech**kee* спички
. . . a lighter	*. . . zazhee**gal**koo* зажигалку
. . . some lighter fluid	*. . . bin**zeen** dlya zazhee**gal**kee* бензин для зажигалки

How much is a packet of tobacco?	***Skol**ka **stoy**eet **pach**ka taba**ka**?* Сколько стоит пачка табака?

At the chemist's

- See also **Health** on page 65.
- Chemist's shops sell simple remedies and medicines, such as aspirin or cough syrup, and a few items such as soap and toothpaste, but they do not stock other toiletries or cosmetics – these can be purchased in specialist shops or department stores. Many chemist's display the sign of a cross, often red. For prescriptions, look out for Дежурная Аптека/*Di**zhoor**naya Ap**tye**ka* (chemist on rota).

I need this medicine	*Mnye **noozh**na eta li**kar**stva* Мне нужно это лекартсво
Can you make up this prescription?	*Viy **mozh**itye preega**to**veet li**kar**stva pa **e**tamoo rit**sep**too?* Вы можете приготовить лекарство по этому рецепту?
When will it be ready?	*Kag**da** a**no** **bood**yet ga**to**va?* Когда оно будет готово?
Please give me ...	***Da**eetye paz**hal**asta ...* Дайте пожалуйста ...
... some cotton wool/gauze	*... **va**too/**marl**yoo* вату/марлю
... a bandage/some plasters	*... beent/**plas**tiyr* бинт/пластырь
... sleeping pills	*... tabl**yet**kee dlya sna* таблетки для сна
... mouth wash/gargle	*... pala**ska**neeye dlya rta/dlya **gor**la* полоскание для рта/ для горла

Have you got something for ...	*Oo vas yist **shto**-neeboot at ...* У вас есть что-нибудь от ...
... a cold	*... **nas**marka* насморка
.. constipation	*... za**po**ra* запора
... a cough	*... **kash**lya* кашля
... diarrhoea	*... po**no**sa* поноса
... hay fever	*... sin**noy** leekha**rat**kee* сенной лихорадки
... a headache	*... galav**noy** **bol**ee* головной боли
... indigestion	*... nisvar**yen**eeya zhi**loot**ka* несварения желудка
... an insect bite	*... oo**koo**sa nasi**kom**ava* укуса насекомого
... nausea	*... tashna**tiy*** тошноты
... stomach upset	*... ras**stroy**stva zhi**loot**ka* расстройства желудка
... sunburn	*... **sol**nichnava a**zho**ga* солнечного ожога

You may hear:

*Preenee**ma**yete li**kar**stvo/ tabl**yet**kee/**kap**lee/para**shok*** Принимайте лекарство/таблетки/ капли/порошок	**Take the medicine/ pills/drops/powder**
*... pa **chai**noy **lozh**kye* по чайной ложке	**... a teaspoonful**

... *dva **ra**za/tree **ra**za f dyen* два раза/три раза в день	**... twice/three times a day**
... ***pos**lye ye**diy**/pye**re**d ye**doy*** после еды/перед едой	**... after meals/before meals**

You may see:

ПРИНИМАЙТЕ КАК УКАЗАНО *Preenee**ma**etye kak oo**ka**zana*	**Take as directed**

Toiletries

Have you got ...?	*Oo vas yist ...?* У вас есть ...?
... soap/shampoo	... ***miy**la/sham**poon*** мыло/шампунь
... a toothbrush/toothpaste	... *zoop**na**ya **shchot**ka/ zoop**na**ya **pa**sta* зубная щётка/ зубная паста
... a (hair) brush/comb	... ***shchot**ka (dlya va**los**)/ grib**yon**ka* щётка (для волос)/ гребёнка
... shaving cream/razor blades	... *kryem dlya breet**ya**/ **lyez**veeya dlya **breet**viy* крем для бритья/ лезвия для бритвы
... sanitary towels/tampons	... *geegeeyen-**tee**cheskeeye salfyetkee/tam**pon**iy* гигиентические сальфетки/тампоны

Photography

Have you got ...?	*Oo vas yist ...?* У вас есть ...?
... a colour film	... *tsvyet**na**ya **plyon**ka* цветная плёнка
... a black and white film	... *chorna-**byel**aya **plyon**ka* чёрно-белая плёнка
... colour slides	... *tsvyet**niy**e deea-pazee**tee**viy* цветные диапозитивы
... a cine film	... *keena**plyon**ka* киноплёнка
Please can you take my photo?	*Pa**zhal**asta, sfata-grafee**roo**eetye min**ya*** Пожалуйста, сфотографируйте меня
I would like to buy ...	*Mne **khoch**itsa koo**peet** ...* Мне хочется купить ...
... a camera	... *fata-appar**at*** фотоаппарат
... a cine camera	... *keena**ka**miroo* кинокамеру
... a light meter	... *ekspa**nom**etr* экспонометр
... a lens	... *abyek**teev*** обьектив
I need some bulbs	*Mnye **noo**zhniy **lam**piy* Мне нужны лампы

MEETING PEOPLE

- Everyone in the Soviet Union has three names: a given name, a patronymic (taken from the father's first name) and surname, e.g. Vitaly Pavlovich (son of Pavel) Shustov. Women's surnames end in **-a**, e.g. Natalia Pavlovna Shustova. There is no way of saying Mr/Mrs/Miss, and the polite equivalent is to address people by their first two names, i.e. given name and patronymic.
- When you are introduced to someone, it is usual to shake hands and to say '***Zdras****tye*/Здравствуйте' (Hello). '***Dob****riy dyen*/Добрый день' (Good day) is used for 'Good afternoon' as well.

What's your name?	*Kak vas za**voot**?* Как вас зовут?
My name is ...	*Mi**nya** za**voot** ...* Меня зовут ...

What's your first name/ patronymic?	*Kak **vashe** **eem**ya/**ot**chestva?* Как ваше имя/ отчество?
How are you?	*Kak viy pazhee**va**yetye?* Как вы поживаете?
Fine, thanks	*Spaseeba, khara**sho*** Спасибо, хорошо
OK	*Nar**mal**na* Нормально
Not bad	*Neeche**vo*** Ничего
Good morning	***Dob**roye **oot**ra* Доброе утро
Good afternoon	***Dob**riy dyen* Добрый день
Good evening	***Dob**riy **vyech**er* Добрый вечер
Good night	*Spa**koy**noy **no**chee* Спокойной ночи
Goodbye	*Da sfee**dan**eeya* До свидания
See you later	*Pa**ka*** Пока
Pleased to meet you	***Och**in pree**yat**na* Очень приятно
Let me introduce you ...	*Pazna**kom**tyes ...* Познакомтесь ...
This is ...	***E**ta ...* Это ...
... my husband/my wife	*... moy moozh/ma**ya** zhe**na*** мой муж/моя жена
... my son/my daughter	*... moy siyn/ma**ya** doch* мой сын/моя дочь
... my sister/my brother	*... ma**ya** sis**tra**/moy brat* моя сестра/мой брат
... my friend	*... moy drook* **(man)**/*ma**ya** pa**droo**ga* **(woman)** мой друг/моя подруга

Allow me to introduce my parents	*Razrisheetye predstaveet maeekh radeetyelyei* Разрешите представить моих родителей
We're together	*Miy fmyestye* Мы вместе
We're staying at ... hotel	*Miy zheevyom f gasteeneetsye ...* Мы живём в гостинице ...
I'm/We're here for the first time	*Ya/Miy zdyes fpyerviy raz* Я/Мы здесь в первый раз
We've been to the Soviet Union before	*Miy oozhe biylee fSavyetskam Sayoozye* Мы уже были в Советском Союзе
once/twice	*adeen raz/dva raza* один раз/два раза
Where are you from?	*Atkooda viy?* Откуда вы?

I'm from ...	*Ya preeyekhal eez* (**man**)/*Ya preeyekhala eez* (**woman**) ... Я приехал из/Я приехала из
We're from ...	*Miy preeyekhalee eez ...* Мы приехали из ...

... London/New York	*... Londana/Nyoo-Yorka* Лондона/Нью-Йорка
... Great Britain	*... Vileekabreetanee'ee* Великобритании
... England/USA	*... Anglee'ee/Saysha* Англии/США
... Canada/Australia	*... Kanadiy/Afstralee'ee* Канады/Австралии

Where do you live?	*Gdye viy zheevyotye?* Где вы живёте?
What's your address/phone number?	*Kakoy vash adryes/tilifon?* Какой ваш адрес/телефон?

Are you married?	*Viy zhe**na**tiy?* **(man)**/ ***za**moozhem?* **(woman)** Вы женаты/замужем?
Have you any children?	*Oo vas yist dit**yei**?* У вас есть детей?
I have … children	*Oo min**ya** … dit**yei*** У меня … детей
I'm single	*Ya ni zhe**nat*** **(man)**/*ni **za**moozhem* **(woman)** Я не женат/не замужем
I'm divorced	*Ya razvid**yon*** **(man)**/ *razvidye**na*** **(woman)** Я разведён/разведена
I like … very much	*Mnye **och**in **nrav**eetsa …* Мне очень нравится …
… Moscow	*… Mask**va*** Москва
… the town	*… etat **gor**at* этот город
… your country	*… **va**sha stra**na*** ваша страна
Please speak slowly	*Gava**reet**ye **myed**linna, pa**zha**lasta* Говорите медленно, пожалуйста
I'm …	*Ya …* Я …
… a businessperson	*… **beez**nismyen* бизнесмен
… an engineer	*… eenzhen**yair*** инженер
… a dentist	*… zoop**noy** vrach* зубной врач
… a doctor	*… vrach* врач

... a pensioner	... *pinseeanyair* (**man**)/ *pinseeanyairka* (**woman**) пенсионер/ пенсионерка
... a student	... *stoodyent* (**man**)/ *stoodyentka* (**woman**) студент/студентка
... a teacher	... *oocheetyel* (**man**)/ *oocheetyelneetsa* (**woman**) учитель/учительница

I'm/We're here on holiday	*Ya/Miy zdyes fotpooskye* Я/Мы здесь в отпуске
I'm here on a business trip	*Ya zdyes f kamandeerofkye* Я здесь в командировке
I'm staying for a week	*Ya astanavleevayoos na nidyelyoo* Я останавливаюсь на неделю
We've been here several days	*Miy zdyes oozhe nyeskalka dnyei* Мы здесь уже несколько дней

Dealing with an invitation

- Russians are generally pleased to meet foreigners, and are very hospitable once you get to know them. Many have learnt to speak some English at school. If you are invited to someone's home, it is nice to take a gift for the host – chocolates, instant coffee, cosmetics, books or magazines, blank cassettes, etc., brought from home will be much appreciated, especially if they come in an attractive carrier-bag.
- Most people live in a block of flats, with the entrance at the back. When finding your way to someone's address, note that дом/*dom* is the name of the building, usually numbered, but it may cover more than one block (корпус/***kor**poos*).
- When arriving at your host's flat (квартира/*kvarteera*), you may be asked to change your shoes

for a pair of slippers. If invited for a meal, you can be certain that elaborate preparations will have been made. The Russians like to entertain guests with the best they can provide by way of food and drink, and at least part of the evening will be spent in proposing toasts and drinking everyone's health.

You may hear:

*Ya kha**choo** preeglas**eet** vas na **ob**yed/na vyecher**eenk**oo/k nam f gos*tee Я хочу вас пригласить на обед/на вечеринку/к нам в гости	**I want to invite you for a meal/to a party/to visit**
*Pree**khod**eetye k nam **zaf**tra/vo **ftor**neek* Приходите к нам завтра/во вторник	**Come over to us tomorrow/on Tuesday**
*Viy sva**bod**niy si**vod**nya **vyech**eram?* Вы свободны сегодня вечером?	**Are you free this evening?**
*Pa-eed**yom**tye fkee**no**/na kant**syert**/pagool**ya**em* Пойдёмте в кино/на концерт/погуляем	**Let's go to the cinema/ a concert/for a walk**
*Kag**da** miy oo**vee**deemsa?* Когда мы увидимся?	**When shall we meet?**

Thank you, I'd be glad to come	*Spas**ee**ba, sooda**vols**tveeyem* Спасибо, с удовольствием
I'm sorry, I can't	***Och**in zhal, no ni ma**goo*** Очень жаль, но не могу
I'm afraid I'm busy	*K sazhal**yen**eeyoo, ya **zan**yat* **(man)**/***zan**yata* **(woman)** К сожалению, я занят/занята
OK, agreed	*Dagavar**ee**lees* Договорились

At someone's house

You may hear:

Meelastee proseem Милости просим	**You're welcome**
Shto viy booditye peet? Что вы будете пить?	**What would you like to drink?**
Davaeetye viypyem za meer/droozhboo Давайте выпьем за мир/дружбу	**Let's drink to peace/ friendship**
Za vashe zdarovye! За ваше здоровье	**Your health!**

You may see:

ДОМ 10 *Dom 10*	**Building no. 10**
КОРПУС 2 *Korpoos 2*	**Block no. 2**
КВАРТИРА 12 *Kvarteera 12*	**Flat 12**

I'll have vodka/wine/coffee	*Ya boodoo peet votkoo/veeno/ kofye* Я буду пить водку/вино/ кофе
This is quite delicious	*Eta prosta prelyest* Это просто прелесть
Did you make it yourself?	*Viy samee gatoveelee eta?* Вы сами готовили это?
Thank you, I'm full	*Spaseeba, ya siyt* **(man)**/*siyta* **(woman)** Спасибо, я сыт/сыта
Thank you for a lovely evening	*Spaseeba za preeyatniy vyecher* Спасибо за приятный вечер
We have to go now	*Nam para* Нам пора

Business appointments

Good morning. My name is ...	***Dob**roye **oot**ra. Min**ya** za**voot** ...* Доброе утро. Меня зовут ...
I represent ...	*Ya pridstav**lya**yoo ...* Я представляю ...
I'm a member of ... organisation/firm	*Ya chlyen ... arganee**zat**see'ee/ **feer**miy* Я член ... организации/ фирмы
Here's my card	*Vot ma**ya** vee**zeet**naya **kart**achka* Вот моя визитная карточка
I have an appointment with ...	*Oo min**ya** naz**nach**ena **fstre**cha s ...* У меня назначена встреча с ...
Here is/are ...	*Vot ...* Вот ...
... our catalogue/our prospectus	*... nash kata**lok**/nash pras**pyekt*** наш каталог/наш проспект
... our price list/our estimate	*... nash pryeiskoo**rant**/**nash**a **smye**ta* наш прейскурант/наша смета
... some samples	*... nyeka**tor**iye ab**raz**tsiy* некоторые образцы
Where is the exhibition hall/ conference hall?	*Gdye **viy**stavachniy zal/ kanfyer**ents**-zal?* Где выставочный зал/ конференц-зал?
I need a translator/guide	*Mnye **noo**zhen piri**vot**cheek/ geed* Мне нужен переводчик/ гид

ESSENTIAL INFORMATION

Emergencies

- The Russian guide or Intourist bureau should be able to help with most minor problems, but for anything more serious, the Embassy can be contacted. In case of accident, the emergency ambulance service can be called, and for car accidents, drivers should contact the traffic police (ГАИ/*GAI*) and obtain a written form for insurance purposes. Embassy addresses in Moscow are as follows:

British Embassy	14 Naberezhnaya Morisa Toreza Tel. 231 85 11; (cultural section) 233 45 07
US Embassy	19–23 Ulitsa Tchaikovskovo Tel. 253 24 51–59
Canadian Embassy	23 Starokonyushenniy Pereulok Tel. 241 91 55
Australian Embassy	13 Kropotkinsky Pereulok Tel. 246 50 11–17
New Zealand Embassy	44 Ulitsa Vorovskovo Tel. 290 12 77

- See also sections **Medical problems** (page 66) and **Problems with the car** (page 86).

Help!	*Na **po**mashch!* На помощь!
Fire!	*Pa**zhar**!* Пожар!
Stop thief!	*Dir**zhee** vora!* Держи вора!
Look out!	*Asta**rozh**na!* Осторожно!
Go away!	*Ooee**deet**ye!* Уйдите!

Call the police/a doctor
*Paza**veet**ye mee**leet**seeyoo/ **vra**cha*
Позовите милицию/врача

Call an ambulance!
***Viy**zaveetye **skor**ooyoo **po**mashch!*
Вызовите скорую помощь!

Where's ...?
Gdye ...?
Где ...?

... the police station
*... atdi**lyen**eeye mee**leet**see'ee*
отделение милиции

... the British Embassy
*... Bree**tan**skoye pa**sol**stva*
Британское посольство

... the American Embassy
*... Amiree**kan**skoye pa**sol**stva*
Американское посольство

I'm lost
*Ya zabloo**deel**sa* **(man)**/*zabloo**deel**as* **(woman)**
Я заблудился/заблудилась

I've lost my wallet
*Ya patir**yal*** **(man)**/*patir**yal**a* **(woman)** *boo**mazh**neek*
Я потеряп/потеряпа бумажник

I've missed the train/plane
*Ya apaz**dal*** **(man)**/*apaz**dal**a* **(woman)** *na **po**yezd/samal**yot***
Я опоздал/опоздала на поезд/самолёт

Someone's stolen ...
*Oo min**ya** oo**kra**lee ...*
У меня украли ...

... my ticket/my handbag
*... beel**yet**/**soo**machkoo*
билет/сумочку

... my luggage/my money
*... ba**gazh**/**dyen**gee*
багаж/деньги

My car has broken down
*Oo min**ya** sla**ma**las ma**shee**na*
У меня сломалась машина

I've had a car accident
*Oo min**ya** biy**la** a**var**eeya*
У меня была авария

Conversion tables

Weights and measures

pounds	lb or kg	kilograms
2.21	1	0.45
4.41	2	0.91
6.61	3	1.36
8.81	4	1.81
11.02	5	2.27
13.22	6	2.72
15.43	7	3.18
17.64	8	3.67
19.83	9	4.08
22.05	10	4.44
44.09	20	9.07
110.23	50	22.68

gallon	l or gal	litre
0.2	1	4.5
0.4	2	9.1
0.7	3	13.6
0.9	4	18.1
1.1	5	22.7
1.3	6	27.2
1.5	7	31.8
1.7	8	36.3
2.0	9	40.9
2.2	10	45.5
4.4	20	90.9
6.6	30	136.3
8.8	40	181.8
11.0	50	227.3

Distance

mile	mile or km	kilometre
0.62	1	1.61
1.24	2	3.22
1.86	3	4.83
2.49	4	6.44
3.11	5	8.05
3.73	6	9.66
4.35	7	11.27
4.97	8	12.87
5.59	9	14.48
6.21	10	19.09
15.54	25	40.23
31.07	50	80.47
62.13	100	160.93
124.27	200	321.86
310.68	500	804.65

Temperature

°F		°C
−22		−30
−4		−20
14		−10
23		−5
32		0
50		10
68		20
85	normal	30
98.4 ←	body →	36.9
122	temperature	50
176		80
212		100

Clothes sizes

- Sizes are different from British, American or Continental. The conversions given here are meant as a rough guide only – it is essential that clothes should be tried on.

Ladies' dresses, etc.

British	10	12	14	16	18
American	8	10	12	14	16
Russian	40	42	44	46	48

Men's collar sizes

British and American	14½	15	15½	16	16½	17
Russian	37	38	39	41	42	43

Shoe and stocking sizes

British	3	4	5	6	7	7½	8	8½	9	9½	10
American	4½	5½	6½	7½	8½	9	9½	10	10½	11	11½
Russian	36	37	38	39	40	41	42		43		44

Numbers

1 ***adeen*** **(m)**/*ad**na*** **(f)**/*ad**no*** **(n)**
один/одна/одно

2 *dva* **(m)**/*dvye* **(f)**
два/две

3 *tree*
три

4 *chi**tiy**re*
четыре

5 *pyat*
пять

6 *shest*
шесть

7 *syem*
семь

8 ***vos**yim*
восемь

9 ***dyev**yat*
девять

10 ***dyes**yat*
десять

11 ***adeen**atsat*
одиннадцать

12 *dvi**nat**sat*
двенадцать

13 *tree**nat**sat*
тринадцать

14 *chi**tiyr**natsat*
четырнадцать

15 *pit**nat**sat*
пятнадцать

16 *shist**nat**sat*
шестнадцать

17 *sim**nat**sat*
семнадцать

18 *vasyim**nat**sat*
восемнадцать

19 *divyat**nat**sat*
девятнадцать

20 ***dvat**sat*
двадцать

m = masculine **f** = feminine **n** = neuter

21 ***dvat**sat **adeen***
двадцать один
22 ***dvat**sat dva*
двадцать два
30 ***treed**sat*
тридцать
40 ***sor**ak*
сорок
50 *pitdis**yat***
пятьдесят
60 *shistdis**yat***
шестьдесят
70 ***syem**disyat*
семьдесят
80 ***vos**yimdisyat*
восемьдесят
90 *divya**nos**ta*
девяносто
100 *sto*
сто
200 ***dvyes**tee*
двести
300 ***tree**sta*
триста
400 *chi**tiy**resta*
четыреста
500 *pyat**sot***
пятьсот
600 *shist**sot***
шестьсот
700 *syim**sot***
семьсот
800 *vasyim**sot***
восемьсот
900 *divyat**sot***
девятьсот
1000 ***tiy**syacha*
тысяча

Ordinal numbers

first ***pyer**viy*
первый

second *f**taroy***
второй

third ***tryet**ee*
третий

fourth *chit**vyor**tiy*
четвёртый

fifth ***pya**tiy*
пятый

sixth *shes**toy***
шестой

seventh *syed**moy***
седьмой

eighth *vas**moy***
восьмой

ninth *div**ya**tiy*
девятый

tenth *dis**ya**tiy*
десятый

eleventh ***adeen**natsatiy*
одиннадцатый

twelfth *dvi**na**tsatiy*
двенадцатый

Public holidays

1 January New Year's Day
8 March Women's Day
1 and 2 May May Day
9 May Victory Day
7 October Constitution Day
7 and 8 November October Revolution Days

Seasons

spring	*vyes**na*** весна	**autumn**	***os**yen* осень
summer	***lyet**a* лето	**winter**	*zee**ma*** зима

Months of the year

January	*yan**var*** январь	**July**	*ee**yool*** июль
February	*fiv**ral*** февраль	**August**	***av**goost* август
March	*mart* март	**September**	*sint**yabr*** сентябрь
April	*apr**yel*** апрель	**October**	*akt**yabr*** октябрь
May	*my* май	**November**	*na**yabr*** ноябрь
June	*ee**yoon*** июнь	**December**	*di**kabr*** декабрь

Days of the week

Monday	*pani**dyel**neek* понедельник	**Friday**	***pya**tneetsa* пятница
Tuesday	***ftor**neek* вторник	**Saturday**	*soo**bot**a* суббота
Wednesday	*sri**da*** среда	**Sunday**	*vaskre**syen**ye* воскресенье
Thursday	*chit**vyerg*** четверг		

Telling the time

What's the time?	*Katoriy chas?* Который час?
It's one o'clock	*Eta chas* Это час
It's 2/3/4 o'clock	*Eta dva/tree/chetiyre chasa* Это два/три/четыре часа
It's five o'clock	*Eta pyat chasof* Это пять часов
... in the morning/ evening	*... ootra/vyechera* утра/вечера
ten past five	*dyesyat meenoot shistova* десять минут шестого
quarter past six	*chetvirt sidmova* четверт седьмого
20 past seven	*dvatsat meenoot vasmova* двадцать минут восьмого
half past eight	*palaveena divyatava* половина девятого
twenty-five to nine	*byez dvatsatee pyatee dyevyat* без двадцати пяти девять
quarter to ten	*byez chetvirtee dyesyat* без четверти десять
five to eleven	*byez pyatee adeennatsat* без пяти одиннадцать
It's midday/midnight	*Eta poldyen/polnach* Это полдень/полночь

Time expressions

today	*sivodnya* сегодня
tomorrow	*zaftra* завтра
yesterday	*fchera* вчера

in the morning — ***oot**ram*
утром

this morning — *si**vod**nya **oot**ram*
сегодня утром

this week — *na etoy ni**dyel**ye*
на этой неделе

last week — *na **prosh**loy ni**dyel**ye*
на прошлой неделе

next week — *na **boo**dooshchei ni**dyel**ye*
на будущей неделе

this year — *f etam ga**doo***
в этом году

last year — *f **prosh**lam ga**doo***
в прошлом году

next year — *f **bood**ooshchem ga**doo***
в будущем году

Countries and nationalities

America — *A**myer**eeka*
Америка

American (man/woman) — *amiree**kan**yets/amiree**kan**ka*
американец/американка

Australia — *Af**stral**eeya*
Австралия

Australian — *afstra**lee**yets/afstra**lee**ka*
австралиец/австралийка

Canada — *Ka**na**da*
Канада

Canadian — *ka**nad**yets/ka**nat**ka*
канадец/канадка

Great Britain — *Vileekabree**tan**eeya*
Великобритания

British — *bree**tan**yets/bree**tan**ka*
британец/британка

USSR — *Sa**vyet**skee Sa**yooz***
Советский Союз

Russian — ***roos**kee/**roos**kaya*
русский/русская

Explanatory note

- **Russian nouns and adjectives**: Nouns in Russian are either masculine, feminine or neuter. Masculine nouns end in a consonant or *i*/й, feminine nouns in *a*/а, *ya*/я or *eeya*/ия, neuter nouns in *o*/о, *ye*/е or *eeye*/ие. Those ending in the soft sign (ь) can be either masculine or feminine. Adjectives take different endings depending on whether the noun is masculine, feminine or neuter (or plural). Masculine endings are generally *iy*/ый or *oy*/ой; feminine endings are *aya*/ая or *yaya*/яя; neuter endings are *oye*/ое or *yeye*/ее. In this wordlist, only the masculine form is given, eg **new** = *noviy*/новый. With a feminine noun, **new** would be ***no**vaya*/ новая, and with a neuter noun, *novoye*/новое.
- **Russian verbs**: These have two infinitives, the imperfective (from which the present tense is formed) and the perfective (which gives the future), e.g. **to say** = *gava**reet***/говорить, *ska**zat***/сказать. The imperfective implies continuing action and the perfective completed action, and different past tenses are formed from these infinitives. In this list, both infinitives are given for the more common verbs; for others, only the imperfective infinitive is listed.

A
address ***adr**yes*/адрес
aeroplane *samal**yot***/ самолёт
after ***pos**lye*/после
agreed *sa**glas**na*/согласно
airport *aera**port***/аэропорт
airmail letter *aveea-pee**smo***/ авиаписьмо
allergy *all**yer**geeya*/ аллергия
to allow *razri**shat***, *razri**sheet***/разрешать, разрешить
along *pa*/по
already *oo**zhe***/уже
amber *yan**tar***/янтарь
ambulance ***skor**aya* ***po**mashch*/скорая помощь
America *Am**yer**eeka*/ Америка
and *ee*/и

another *droo**goy***/другой; (**more**) *yish**cho** a**deen***/ещё один
antique *sta**reen**niy*/ старинный
anyone ***kto**-ta*/кто-то
apple ***yab**laka*/яблоко
  apple juice ***yab**lachniy sok*/яблочный сок
appointment *naz**na**chena fstre**cha***/назначена встреча
  to make an appointment with *zapee**sat**sa s*/ записаться с
arm *roo**ka***/рука
arrival *pree**biy**teeye*/ прибытие
to arrive *preekha**deet**, pree**tee***/приходить, прийти
art *ees**koost**va*/исскуство
  art gallery *kar**teen**naya galir**ye**ya*/картинная галерея
artist *khoo**dozh**neek*/ художник
as *kak*/как
at *f*/в, *oo*/у
  at once *syei**chas***/сейчас
to ask *spraShee**vat**, spra**seet***/спрашивать, спросить
ashtray ***pyep**ilneetsa*/ пепельница
Australia *Af**stra**leeya*/ Австралия

B
back (body) *spee**na***/спина
  (direction) *a**brat**na*/ обратно
bad *pla**khoy***/плохой
bag ***soom**ka*/сумка
baker's ***boo**lachnaya*/ булочная
ball (tennis etc.) *myach*/мяч
balcony *bal**kon***/балкон
ballet *bal**yet***/балет
bandage *beent*/бинт
bank *bank*/банк
bar *bar*/бар
bath ***van**na*/ванна
  bathroom ***van**naya*/ ванная
to bathe *koo**pat**sa*/купаться
bathing costume *koo**pal**niy kast**yoom***/купальный костюм
battery *batir**ye**ya*/батерея
to be *biyt*/быть
beach *plyazh*/пляж
beard *bara**da***/борода
beautiful *kra**see**viy*/ красивый
because *pata**moo** shto*/ потому что
bed *kra**vat***/кровать; *past**yel***/постель
beef *gav**ya**deena*/говядина
beer ***pee**va*/пиво
before ***pye**red*/перед
to begin *nachee**nat**(sa), na**chat**(sa)*/начинать(ся), начать(ся)
beginning *na**cha**la*/начало
bell *zva**nok***/звонок
belt ***po**yis*/пояс
better ***looch**shee*/лучший
bicycle *velasee**pyet***/ велосипед
big *bal**shoy***/большой
bill *sshot*/счёт
binoculars *bee**nokl***/бинокль
black ***chor**niy*/чёрный
blanket *ade**ya**la*/одеяло
blind (window) ***shto**ra*/штора
blood *krof*/кровь
blouse ***blooz**ka*/блузка
blue (light) *galoo**boy***/ голубой
  (dark) ***see**nee*/синий
boat ***lot**ka*/лодка
  (motor) *tipla**khot***/ теплоход
  (steam) *para**khot***/ пароход
book ***knee**ga*/книга
to book *za**ka**ziyvat, zaka**zat***/заказывать, заказать
booking office ***kas**sa*/касса

boots *sapa**gee***/сапоги
border *gra**neet**sa*/граница
bottle *boo**tiyl**ka*/бутылка
box *ka**rop**ka*/коробка; (**theatre**) ***lo**zha*/ложа
brandy *kan**yak***/коньяк
bread *khlyep*/хлеб
to break *la**mat**, sla**mat***/ ломать, сломать
to break down (car) *sla**mat**sa*/сломаться
breakfast ***zaf**trak*/завтрак
to have breakfast ***zaf**trakat*/завтракать
bridge *most*/мост
British *breet**an**skee*/ британский
to bring *preena**seet**, preenis**tee***/приносить, принести
brother *brat*/брат
brown *ka**reech**nyeviy*/ коричневый
brush ***shchot**ka*/щётка
bus *af**to**boos*/автобус
bus stop *asta**nof**ka af**to**boosa*/остановка автобуса
business ***dye**la*/дело
on business *pa dye**lam***/по делам
business person ***bee**znismyen*/бизнесмен
business trip *kamandee**rof**ka*/ командировка
busy ***zan**yatiy*/занятый
but *no*/но
butter ***mas**la*/масло
button ***poo**gaveetsa*/ пуговица
to buy *pakoo**pat**, koo**peet***/ покупать, купить

C

cabbage *ka**poos**ta*/капуста
cake *pee**rozh**noye*/ пирожное
to be called *naziy**vat**sa*/ называться
camera *fata-appa**rat***/ фотоаппарат
camp bed *pa**khod**niy kra**vat***/походный кровать
camp-site ***kem**peeng*/ кемпинг
can (I can, one can etc.) ***mozh**na*/можно
Canada *Ka**na**da*/Канада
car *ma**shee**na*/машина, *aftama**beel***/автомобиль (**m**)
car park *sta**yan**ka aftama**beel**yei*/стоянка автомобилей
caravan *dom-aftafoor**gon***/ дом-автофургон
card ***kar**tachka*/карточка
visiting card *vee**zeet**naya* .../ визитная ...
credit ... *kre**deet**naya* .../ кредитная ...
cards (**playing**) ***kar**tiy*/ карты
cardigan ***kof**tachka*/ кофточка
to carry (**luggage**) *atna**seet**, atnyes**tee***/относить, отнести
cash desk ***kas**sa*/касса
castle ***za**mak*/замок
cathedral *sa**bor***/собор
caviar *ee**kra***/икра
centre *tsentr*/центр
century *vyek*/век
chair *stool*/стул
champagne *sham**pan**skoye*/ шампанское
change (**money**) ***sda**cha*/ сдача
(**small**) ***mye**lach*/мелочь
to change (**money**) *abmin**yat**, abmi**neet***/обменять, обменить
(**sheets**) *pirimin**yat***/ переменять
(**zip, bulb**) *zamin**yat***/ заменять
(**trains**) ***dye**lat piri**sat**koo*/ делать пересадку

cheap *dishoviy*/дешёвый
to check (bill etc.) *praviryat*/ проверять
check-in (air) *rigeestratseeya*/ регистрация
cheese *siyr*/сыр;
 cottage ... *tvorok*/ творог
chemist's *aptyeka*/аптека
cheque *chek*/чек
cherry *veeshnya*/вишня
chess *shakhmatiy*/шахматы
chest (body) *groot*/грудь
chicken *kooreetsa*/курица
child *ribyonak*/ребёнок
children *dyetee*/дети
chocolate *shakalat*/шоколад
 bar of chocolate *pleetka shakalada*/плитка шоколада
to choose *viybeerat*, *viybrat*/ выбирать, выбрать
church *tsyerkaf*/церковь
cigar *seegara*/сигара
cigarette *seegaryeta*/ сигарета;
 (Russian) *papeerosa*/ папироса
cinema *keeno*/кино
clean *cheestiy*/чистый
to clean *cheesteet*/чистить
cloakroom *gardyirop*/ гардероб
clock *chasiy*/часы
to close *zakriyvat*(*sa*), *zakriyt*(*sa*)/закрывать(ся), закрыть(ся)
closed *zakriyta*/закрыто
clothing *adyezhda*/одежда
coat *palto*/падьто
coathanger *vyeshalka*/ вешалка
coffee *kofye*/кофе
cold *khalodniy*/холодный
cold (med.) *nasmork*/насморк; *prastooda*/простуда
collar *varatneek*/воротник
colour *tsvyet*/цвет
comb *gribyonka*/гребёнка

to come *preekhodeet*, *preetee*/приходить, прийти
 come in! *vaeedeetye*!/ войдите!
 to come back *vazvrashchatsa*, *virnootsa*/ возвращаться, вернуться
compartment (train) *koopay*/ купе
concert *kantsyert*/концерт
constipation *zapor*/запор
conversation *razgavor*/ разговор
copy *kopeeya*/копия
corkscrew *shtopar*/штопор
to cost *stoyeet*/стоить
cotton *neetka*/нитка
cotton wool *vata*/вата
cough *kashel*/кашель
country *strana*/страна
countryside *diryevnya*/ деревня
cream *sleefkee*/сливки
 sour cream *smetana*/ сметана
crossing (street etc) *pirikhot*/ переход
cucumber *agooryets*/огурец
cup *chashka*/чашка
currency (foreign) *valyoota*/ валюта
customs *tamozhnya*/ таможня
to cut *ryezat*/резать
 (hair) *padstreegat*/ подстригать

D

to dance *tantsivat*/ танцевать
dangerous *apasniy*/опасный
date *cheeslo*/число
daughter *doch*/дочь **(f)**
day *dyen*/день
dear *daragoy*/дорогой
to declare *zayavlyat*, *zayaveet*/заявлать, заявить
dentist *zoopnoy vrach*/ зубной врач

department *atdyel*/отдел
department store *ooneevyermak*/универмаг
dessert *disyert*/десерт
dictionary *slavar*/словарь
diarrhoea *panos*/понос
difficult *troodniy*/трудный
dining-room *stalovaya*/столовая
direct (train) *pryamoy*/прямой
direction *napraylyeneeya*/направления
dirty *gryazniy*/грязный
divorced *razvidyonniy*/разведённый
to do *dyelat, sdyelat*/делать, сделать
doctor *vrach*/врач; *doktar*/доктор
doll *kookla*/кукла
dollar *dollar*/доллар
downstairs *vneezoo*/внизу
to draw *reesavat*/рисовать
dress *platye*/платье
to drink *peet, viypeet*/пить, выпить
dry *sookhoy*/сухой
dry cleaning *kheemcheestka*/химчистка
duty (customs) *poshleena*/пошлина

E

ear *ookha*/ухо; **ears** *ooshee*/уши
early *rana*/рано
earrings *syergee*/серьги
east *vastok*/восток
to eat *yist*/есть
egg *yaitsa*/яйцо; **eggs** *yaitsa*/яйца
embassy *pasolstva*/посольство
engaged (taken) *zanyata*/занято
England *Angleeya*/Англия
English *angleeskee*/английский
enough *dastatachna*/достаточно
entrance *fkhot*/вход
envelope *kanvyert*/конверт
equipment *abaroodavaneeye*/оборудование
evening *vyecher*/вечер
every *kazhdiy*/каждый
excursion *ekskoorseeya*/экскурсия; *payezdka*/поездка
excuse me *eezveeneetye*/извините
exhibition *viystafka*/выставка
exit *viykhat*/выход
to explain *abyisnyat*/объяснять
eye *glaz*/глаз; **eyes** *glaza*/глаза

F

face *leetso*/лицо
to fall *padat, oopast*/падать, упасть
famous *znameneetiy*/знаменитый
far *daliko*/далеко
father *atyets*/отец
to feel *choostvavat*/чувствовать
I feel *ya choostvooyo sibya*/я чувствую себя
fever *leekharatka*/лихорадка
to fill in (form) *zapalnyat, zapolneet*/заполнять, заполнить
filling (dental) *plomba*/пломба
film (cinema) *feelm*/фильм
colour film *tsvitnaya plyonka*/цветная плёнка
fine *prekrasniy*/прекрасный
finger *palyits*/палец
to finish *kanchat(sa), koncheet(sa)*/кончать(ся), кончить(ся)
fire *pazhar*/пожар
fish *riyba*/рыба
flat (apartment) *kvarteera*/квартира
flight *ryeis*/рейс

floor (storey) *etazh*/этаж
flower *tsvitok*/цветок
flu *greep*/грипп
fog *tooman*/туман
food *pradooktiy*/продукты
foot *naga*/нога;
on ... *pishkom*/пешком
for *dlya*/для
fork *veelka*/вилка
free *svabodniy*/свободный
fresh *svezhee*/свежий
friend *drook* **(m)**, *padrooga* **(f)**/друг, подруга
from *at*/от
(out of) *eez*/из
fruit *frookt*/фрукт
fruit juice *frooktoviy sok*/ фруктовый сок
fur *myekh*/мех

G

garden *sat*/сад
gentlemen's (toilet) *moozhskoy twalyet*/ мужской туалет
genuine *nastayashchee*/ настоящий
to get off, out *viykhadeet*/ выходить
girl *dyevooshka*/девушка
to give *davat*, *dat*/давать, дать
give! *daeetye!*/дайте!
glass *stakan*/стакан
glasses *achkee*/очки
gloves *pirchatkee*/перчатки
to go (on foot) *eetee*, *paeetee*/идти, пойти
(by transport) *yekhat*, *payekhat*/ехать, поехать
gold *zolata*/золото
good *kharoshee*/хороший
goodbye *da sfeedaneeya*/до свидания
grapes *veenagrat*/виноград
grateful *blagadarniy*/ благодарный
Great Britain *Vileeka-breetaneeya*/ Великобритания
green *zilyoniy*/зелёный
grey *syeriy*/серый
group *groppa*/группа
guide *geed*/гид
guidebook *pootivadeetyel*/ путеводитель

H

hair *volasiy*/волосы
hair dryer *soosheelka*/ сушилка
hairdresser's *pareekmakhirskaya*/ парикмахерская
half *palaveena*/половина
hall *zal*/зал
ham *vitcheena*/ветчина
hand *rooka*/рука
handbag *soomachka*/ сумочка
handkerchief *nasavoy platok*/носовой платок
hat *shlyapa*/шляпа
I have *oo minya yist*/у меня есть
do you have? *oo vas yist?*/ у вас есть?
you have to *vam nada*/ вам надо
he *on*/он
head *galava*/голова
headache *galavnaya bol*/ головная боль **(f)**
heart *syertse*/сердце
heating *ataplyeneeye*/ отопление
hello *zdrastye*/ здравствуйте
help *pomashch*/помощь
to help *pamagat*, *pamoch*/ помогать, помочь
her *yeyo*/её
here *zdyes*/здесь
here is/are *vot*/вот
high *viysokee*/высокий
to hire *vzyat naprokat*/ взять напрокат
his *yevo*/его
hole *diyrka*/дырка
on holiday *fotpooskye*/в отпуске

hospital *bal**neet**sa*/больница
hot *gar**ya**chee*/горячий
hotel *gas**teen**eetsa*/ гостиница
hotel pass ***pro**poosk*/ пропуск
hour *chas*/час
house *dom*/дом
how *kak*/как
how much/many ***skol**ka*/ сколько
hungry *ga**lod**niy*/голодный
to hurry *spi**shat**, spi**sheet***/ спешать, спешить
I'm in a hurry *ya spi**shoo***/я спешу
my ... hurts *oo min**ya** ba**leet** ...*/у меня болит ...
husband *moozh*/муж

I

I *ya*/я
ice *lyot*/лёд
ice cream *ma**ro**zhenaye*/ мороженое
if ***yes**lee*/если
ill *bal**noy***/больной
important ***vazh**niy*/важный
in, into *f*/в
information ***spraf**kee*/ справки
injection ***oo**kal*/укол
to introduce *predstav**lyat***/ представлять
to iron ***gla**deet*/гладить
insect *nasi**ko**moye*/ насекомое
insect repellant ***sred**stva nasi**ko**mava*/средство насекомого
insect bite *oo**koos** nasi**ko**mava*/укус насекомого
insurance *stra**khof**ka*/ страховка
international *mizhdoona**rod**niy*/ международный
interpreter *piri**vot**cheek* /переводчик
interval *antr**akt***/антракт
to invite *preegla**shat***, preegla**seet**/приглашать, пригласить
Ireland *Eeer**lan**deeya*/ Ирландия
Irish *eer**land**skee*/ ирландский
it ***e**ta*/это

J

jacket ***koort**ka*/куртка
jam *va**ren**ye*/варенье
jar ***ban**ka*/банка
jeweller's *yoovi**leer**niy maga**zeen***/ювелирный магазин
job *ra**bo**ta*/работа
journey *pa**yezd**ka*/поездка
juice *sok*/сок

K

key *klyooch*/ключ
kind ***dob**riy*/добрый
kiosk *kee**osk***/киоск
newspaper kiosk *gaz**yet**niy kee**osk***/газетный киоск
knee *kal**yen**a*/колено
knife *nozh*/нож
to know *znat*/знать
I know *ya **zna**yoo*/я знаю
do you know? *viy **zna**etye*?/вы знаете?

L

lace ***kroo**zheva*/кружево
ladies' (toilet) ***zhen**skee twal**yet***/женский туалет
lake ***oz**yera*/озеро
lamb *ba**ra**neena*/баранина
lamp ***lam**pa*/лампа
language *ya**ziyk***/язык
last *pas**lyed**nee*/последний
to be late *a**paz**diyvatsa*/ опаздываться
leather ***ko**zha*/кожа
to leave (car) *pastav**lyat***/ поставлять

(valuables) *astavlyat*/ оставлять
to leave (set out) *atpravlyatsa, atpraveetsa*/ отправляться, отправиться
(train) *atkhodeet*/ отходить
left *lyeviy*/левый
on the left *nalyeva*/ налево
leg *naga*/нога
lemon *leemon*/лимон
lemonade *leemanat*/ лимонад
letter *peesmo*/письмо
lettuce *salat*/салат
lift (elevator) *leeft*/лифт
light *svyet*/свет
light bulb *lampachka*/ лампочка
lighter *zazheegalka*/ зажигалка
I like *mnye nraveetsa*/мне нравится
I would like *ya khatyel (khatyela) biy* [**m**, (*f*)]/ я хотел (хотела) бы
lip *gooba*/губа
lipstick *goobnaya pamada*/ губная помада
to listen *slooshat, paslooshat*/слушать, послушать
litre *leetr*/литр
little *malinkee*/маленький
a little *nimnoga*/немного
to live *zheet*/жить
lock *zamok*/замок
long *dleenniy*/длинный
to look at *smatryet, pasmatryet*/смотреть, посмотреть
to look for *eeskat*/искать
lorry *groozaveek*/грузовик
to lose *tiryat, patiryat*/ терять, потерять
to be lost *zabloodatsa, zabloodeetsa*/заблудаться, заблудиться
lost property office *byooro nakhodak*/бюро находок
loud *gromkee*/громкий
to love *lyoobeet*/любить
luggage *bagazh*/багаж
left luggage office *kamira khranyeneeya*/камера хранения
lunch *abyed*/обед
to have lunch *abyedat* /обедать

M

magazine *zhoornal*/журнал
main *glavniy*/главный
to make *dyelat, sdyelat*/ делать, сделать
makeup *kasmyeteeka*/ косметика
man *moozhcheena*/мужчина
manager *admeeneestratar*/ администратор
many *mnoga*/много
map *karta*/карта
market *riynak*/рынок
married (man) *zhenatiy*/ женатый
(woman) *zamoozhem*/ замужем
match (game) *eegra*/игра
football match *footbolniy match*/футбольный матч
matches (fire) *speechkee*/ спички
mayonnaise *mayanez*/ майонез
me *minya*/меня
to me *mnye*/мне
meat *myasa*/мясо
medicine *likarstva*/ лекарстсво
meeting *fstrecha*/встреча
to meet *fstrechat, fstreteet*/ встречать, встретить
to mend *cheeneet*/чинить
menu *minyoo*/меню
message *zapeeska*/записка
middle *sirideena*/середина
milk *malako*/молоко

mineral water *meene**ral**naya va**da***/минеральная вода
minute *mee**noo**ta*/минута
mirror ***zyer**kala*/зеркало
mistake *a**sheep**ka*/ошибка
money ***dyen**gee*/деньги
month ***myes**yats*/месяц
monument ***pam**yatneek*/ памятник
moon *loo**na***/луна
more *yish**cho***/ещё
morning ***oot**ra*/утро
in the morning ***oot**ram*/ утром
mother *mat*/мать
mountain *ga**ra***/гора
moustache *oo**siy***/усы
mouth *rot*/рот
museum *mooz**yei***/музей
mushroom *greep*/гриб
music ***moo**ziyka*/музыка
I must (man) *ya **dol**zhin*/я должен
(woman) *ya dalzh**na***/я должна
my *moy* **(m)**, *ma**ya*** **(f)**, *ma**yo*** **(n)**, *maee* **(pl)**/мой, моя, моё, мои
myself *sib**ya***/себя

N

nail (finger) ***no**gat*/ноготь
nail file ***peel**ka dlya nak**tyei***/пилка для ногтей
name (first) ***eem**ya*/имя
(surname) *fa**mee**leeya*/ фамилия
nappy *pil**yon**ka*/пелёнка
narrow ***ooz**kee*/узкий
near ***bleez**kee*/близкий
nearest *blee**zha**eeshee*/ ближайший
nearly *pach**tee***/почти
neck ***she**ya*/шея
necklace *ozhir**yel**ye*/ ожерелье
I need *mnye **noozh**na*/мне нужно
needle *ee**gol**ka*/иголка
never *neekag**da***/никогда
new ***no**viy*/новый
newspaper *ga**zye**ta*/газета
newspaper kiosk *ga**zyet**niy kee**osk***/газетный киоск
New Zealand ***No**vaya Zi**lan**deeya*/Новая Зеландия
next ***slye**dooyooshchee*/ следующий
next to ***rya**dam s*/рядом с
night *noch*/ночь **(f)**
no *nyet*/нет
no one *nee**kto***/никто
noisy ***shoom**niy*/шумный
north ***sye**vir*/север
nose *nos*/нос
not *ni*/не
nothing *neeche**vo***/ничего
now *tip**yair***/теперь
number *chees**lo***/число; **(room)** ***no**mir*/номер
nurse *midsis**tra***/медсестра

O

occupied ***zan**yatiy*/занятый
office *kan**to**ra*/контора
often ***chas**ta*/часто
oil ***mas**la*/масло
old ***sta**riy*/старый
on, onto *na*/на
only ***tol**ka*/только
open *at**kriy**ta*/открыто
to open *atkriy**vat**(sa)*, *at**kriyt**(sa)*/открывать(ся), открыть(ся)
opera ***o**pira*/опера
opposite ***pro**teev*/против
or ***ee**lee*/или
orange (fruit) *apyil**seen***/ апельсин
orange juice *apyil**seen**aviy sok*/апельсиновый сок
(colour) *a**ran**zheviy*/ оранжевый
orchestra *ark**yestr***/оркестр
to order *za**ka**ziyvat*, *zaka**zat***/заказывать, заказать
to organise *arganee**zee**ravat*/ организировать
other *droo**goy***/другой

our *nash* (**m**), ***na**sha* (**f**), ***na**she* (**n**), ***na**shee* (**pl**)/наш, наша, наше, наши
out of *eez*/из
over *nad*/над

P
packet (**parcel**) *pak**yet***/ пакет, *bandi**rol***/бандероль (f) (**butter etc**) ***pach**ka*/пачка
pain *bol*/боль (f)
painkiller ***bo**lye-ootal**ya**yooshcheye*/ болеутоляющее
paper *boo**ma**ga*/бумага
parcel *pa**siyl**ka*/посылка
parents *ra**deet**yelee*/ родители
park *park*/парк
to park (**car**) *pastav**lyat** ma**shee**noo*/поставлять машину
party *vyechere**een**ka*/ вечеринка
passport ***pas**part*/паспорт
to pay *pla**teet**, zapla**teet***/ платить, заплатить
peach ***pyer**seek*/персик
pear ***groo**sha*/груша
pen ***rooch**ka*/ручка
pencil *karan**dash***/карандаш
pepper ***pyer**its*/перец
performance *spik**takl***/ спектакль
perfume *doo**khee***/духи
perhaps ***mo**zhit biyt*/может быть
person *chila**vyek***/человек
petrol *bin**zeen***/бензин
petrol station *benzaka**lon**ka*/ бензоколонка
photograph *fata**gra**feeya*/ фотография
to take a photograph *fatagra**fee**ravat*/ фотографировать
pie *peera**zhok***/пирожок, *pee**rok***/пирог
piece ***koo**sak*/кусок
pill *tabl**yet**ka*/таблетка
pillow *pa**doosh**ka*/подушка
pillowcase *nava**loch**ka*/ наволочка
pink ***ro**zaviy*/розовый
place ***myes**ta*/место
plate *tar**yel**ka*/тарелка
plaster (**med.**) ***plas**tiyr*/ пластырь
platform *plat**for**ma*/ платформа; *per**ron***/перрон
play (**theatre**) ***pye**sa*/пьеса
to play *ee**grat***/играть
pleasant *pree**yat**niy*/ приятный
please *pa**zhal**asta*/ пожалуйста
with pleasure *sooda**vol**stveeyem*/с удовольствием
plug (**elec.**) ***shtyep**silnaya **veel**ka*/штепсельная вилка (**sink**) ***prop**ka*/пробка
plum ***slee**va*/слива
police *mee**leet**seeya*/ милиция
policeman *meeleetseeyan**yair***/ милиционер
police station *atdil**yen**eeye mee**leet**see'ee*/отделение милиции
pond *proot*/пруд
pork *svee**nee**na*/свинина
porter *na**seel**shcheek*/ носильщик
is it possible ***mozh**na?*/ можно?
post box *pach**to**viy **yash**cheek*/почтовый ящик
post office ***poch**ta*/почта
postcard *at**kriyt**ka*/ открытка
poste restante ***poch**ta da vas**tryeb**avaneeya*/почта до востребования
poster *pla**kat***/плакат
potato *kar**tosh**ka*/картошка
pound (**money**) *foont*/фунт
prescription *rit**sept***/рецепт
present *pa**da**rak*/подарок

price *tse**na***/цена
private ***chast**niy*/частный
probably *vera**yat**na*/ вероятно
problem *prab**lyem**a*/ проблема
profession *praf**yes**seeya*/ профессия
programme *pra**gram**ma*/ программа
pump *na**sos***/насос
purse *kashel**yok***/кошелёк
pyjamas *pee**zha**ma*/пижама

Q
quarter ***chet**virt*/четверть
question *va**pros***/вопрос
quick(ly) ***biy**stra*/быстро; *skar**ye**ye*/скорее
quiet ***teek**hee*/тихий
quite *sav**syem***/совсем

R
racket *rak**yet**ka*/ракетка
radiator *radee**a**tar*/ радиатор
radio ***ra**deeo*/радио
railway *zhil**yez**naya da**ro**ga*/ железная дорога
it is raining *dozhd eed**yot***/ дождь идёт
raincoat *plashch*/плащ
rash (med.) *siyp*/сыпь
rate of exchange *val**yoot**niy koors*/валютный курс
raw *siy**roy***/сырой
razor ***breet**va*/бритва
razor blades ***lyez**veeya dlya **breet**viy*/лезвия для бритвы
ready *ga**to**viy*/готовый
real *nasta**yash**chee*/ настоящий
recently *nidav**no***/недавно
receipt *kvee**tant**seeya*/ квитанция
to recommend *rikam**yen**davat*/ рекомендовать
record *plas**teen**ka*/ пластинка

red ***kras**niy*/красный
reduction ***skeet**ka*/скидка
refrigerator *khala**deel**neek*/ холодильник
registered *zakaz**niy***/ заказный
registered letter *zakaz**no**ye pees**mo***/заказное письмо
to rent *nanee**mat***/нанимать
to repair *(at)riman**tee**ravat*/ (от)ремонтировать
to repeat *paftar**yat***, *pafta**reet***/повторять, повторить
to reply *atvi**chat***, *at**vyet**eet*/ отвечать, ответить
reservation *za**kaz***/заказ
to reserve *za**ka**ziyvat*, *zaka**zat***/заказывать, заказать
restaurant *rista**ran***/ ресторан
restaurant car *va**gon**-rista**ran***/вагон-ресторан
rice *rees*/рис
right ***pra**viy*/правый
on the right *na**pra**va*/ направо
right (correct) ***pra**veelniy*/правильный
ring (jewel.) *kalt**so***/кольцо
river *rye**ka***/река
road *da**ro**ga*/дорога
roll (bread) ***boo**lachka*/булочка
room ***kom**nata*/комната
(hotel) ***no**mir*/номер
row (line) *ryat*/ряд
rubber *ri**zeen**ka*/резинка
rubbish ***moo**sar*/мусор
rubbish bin ***moo**sarniy **yash**cheek*/мусорный ящик
Russia *Ras**see**ya*/Россия
Russian ***roo**skee* **(m)**/ русский, ***roo**skaya* **(f)**/ русская

S
safe (box) *syeif*/сейф
(secure) *byeza**pas**niy*/ безопасный

salad *sal**at***/салад
salami sausage *kalba**sa***/колбаса
sale *pra**da**zha*/продажа
salmon *lasa**seena***/ лососина;
smoked ... ***syom**ga*/ сёмга
salt *sol*/соль
salty *sal**yon**iy*/солёный
samovar *sama**var***/самовар
sand *pi**sok***/песок
sandwich *booter**brot***/ бутерброд
sanitary towel *geegee-en**tee**cheskaya sal**fyet**ka*/ гигиентическая салфетка
sausage *sa**sees**ka*/сосиска
to say *gava**reet**, ska**zat***/ говорить, сказать
scarf *sharf*/шарф
head scarf *pla**tok***/платок
scissors ***nozh**neetsiy*/ ножницы
Scotland *Shat**lan**deeya*/ Шотландия
Scottish *shat**land**skee*/ шотландский
sea ***mor**ye*/море
seat ***myes**ta*/место
second (time) *se**koon**da*/ секунда
to see ***veed**yet, oo**veed**yet*/ видеть, увидеть
(sights) *smat**ryet***, *pasmat**ryet***/смотреть, посмотреть
to sell *prada**vat**, pra**dat***/ продавать, продать
to send *pasiy**lat**, pas**lat***/ посылать, послать
serious *sir**yoz**niy*/серёзный
service (church) ***slooz**hba*/ служба
self-service *sama-ap**sloo**zheevaneeye*/ самообслуживание
to sew *sheet*/шить
shampoo *sham**poon***/ шампунь
sharp ***os**triy*/острый
shaving cream *krem dlya breet**ya***/крем для бритья
she *a**na***/она
sheet *pras**tiy**nya*/простыня
shirt *roo**bash**ka*/рубашка
shoes ***toof**lee*/туфли
shop *maga**zeen***/магазин; ***laf**ka*/лавка
short *ka**rot**kee*/короткий
shoulder *pli**cho***/плечо
to show *pa**ka**ziyvat, paka**zat***/показывать, показать
shower *doosh*/душ
to shut *zakriy**vat**(sa), za**kriyt**(sa)*/закрывать(ся), закрыть(ся)
shut *za**kri**yta*/закрыто
I feel sick *min**ya** tash**neet***/ меня тошнит
side *stara**na***/сторона
sights *dastapreemi-**cha**tilnastee*/ достопримечательности
sign *znak*/знак
signpost *ooka**zat**yel*/ указатель
to sign (form) *ras**pee**siyvat*/расписывать
sink ***ra**kaveena*/раковина
silver *siri**bro***/серебро
sister *sis**tra***/сестра
to sit ***seed**yet*/сидеть
size *raz**myer***/размер
skates *kan**kee***/коньки
to skate *kat**at**sa na kan**kakh***/кататься на коньках
skating rink *ka**tok***/каток
skis ***liyzh**ee*/лыжи
to ski *kha**deet** na **liyzh**akh*/ ходить на лыжах
skirt ***yoop**ka*/юбка
sky ***nyeba***/небо
to sleep *spat*/спать
sleeping bag *sp**al**niy mi**shok***/ спальный мешок
sledge ***sa**nee*/сани
slippers ***ta**pachkee*/тапочки

slow *myedlinniy*/медленный
slowly *myedlinna*/медленно
smell *zapakh*/запах
to smoke *kooreet*/курить
snack *zakooska*/закуска
snow *snyek*/снег
so *tak*/так
soap *miyla*/мыло
socks *naskee*/носки
soft *myakhkee*/мягкий
someone *kto-ta*/кто-то
something *shto-ta*/што-то
sometimes *eenagda*/иногда
somewhere *gdye-ta*/где-то
son *siyn*/сын
song *pyesnya*/песня
soon *skora*/скоро
soup *soop*/суп
sorry (man) *veenavat*/виноват; **(woman)** *veenavata*/виновата
south *yook*/юг
souvenir *soovineer*/сувенир
Soviet Union *Savyetskee Sayooz*/Советский Союз
spare *leeshnee*/лишний
spare parts *zapchastee*/запчасти
to speak *gavareet*/говорить
do you speak? *viy gavareetye ...?*/вы говорите ...?
spoon *lozhka*/ложка
spring (season) *vyesna*/весна
square *ploshchat*/площадь
Red Square *Krasnaya ploshchat*/Красная площадь
stadium *stadeeon*/стадион
stain *pyitno*/пятно
staircase *lyestneetsa*/лестница
stale *nisvyezhee*/несвежий
stalls (theatre) *partyair*/партер
stamp *marka*/марка; **stamps** *markee*/марки
to stand *stayat*/стоять
starters *zakooskee*/закуски
station *stantseeya*/станция
(main) *vakzal*/вокзал
to stay *astanavleevatsa, astanaveetsa*/останавливаться, остановиться
(in hotel) *zheet*/жить
steak *beefshteks*/бифштекс
to steal *krast*/красть
still *yishcho*/ещё
stockings *choolkee*/чулки
stomach *zhiloodak*/желудок
stone *kamyen*/камень
to stop *astanavleevatsa*/останавливаться
storm *graza*/гроза
straight on *pryama*/прямо
strap *rimishok*/ремешёк
street *ooleetsa*/улица
string *viryofka*/верёвка
strong *seelniy*/сильный
student *stoodyent* **(m)**/студент; *stoodyentka* **(f)**/студентка
suddenly *fdrook*/вдруг
sugar *sakhar*/сахар
suitcase *chemadan*/чемодан
summer *lyeta*/лето
sun *sontse*/солнце
sun stroke *solnichniy oodar*/солнечный удар
supermarket *ooneeversam*/универсам
supper *oozheen*/ужин
to have supper *oozheenat*/ужинать
sweater *sveetyair*/свитер
sweet *slatkee*/сладкий
sweets *kanfyetiy*/конфеты
to swim *koopatsa*/купаться
swimming pool *plavatilniy bassyein*/плавательный бассейн
to switch off *viyklyoocheet*/выключить
to switch on *fklyoocheet*/включить

T

table *stol*/стол
(in restaurants) *staleek*/столик
tablecloth *skatyert*/скатерть
to take *brat*, *vzyat*/брать, взять
(pills etc.) *preenaseet*, *preenyestee*/приносить, принести
tall *viysokee*/высокий
tampon *tampon*/тампон
tap *kran*/кран
tasty *fkoosniy*/вкусный
taxi *taksee*/такси
taxi rank *stayanka taksee*/стоянка такси
tea *chay*/чай
teacher (man) *oocheetyel*/учитель
(woman) *oocheetyelneetsa*/учительница
team *kamanda*/команда
telegram *tiligramma*/телеграмма
telegram form *blank tiligrammiy*/бланк телеграммы
telephone *tilifon*/телефон
telephone number *nomir tilifona*/номер телефона
to telephone *zvaneet*, *pazvaneet*/звонить, позвонить
television *tiliveezar*/телевизор
to tell *rasskaziyvat*/рассказывать
temperature *timpiratoora*/температура
tennis *tyennees*/теннис
tent *palatka*/палатка
thank you *spaseeba*/спасибо
that *tot* **(m)**, *ta* **(f)**, *to* **(n)**/тот, та, то
theatre *tiyatr*/театр
their *eekh*/их
then *tagda*/тогда
there *tam*/там;
… is, are *yist*/есть
these *etee*/эти
they *anee*/они
thing *vyeshch*/вещь **(f)**
to think *doomat*/думать
I am thirsty *mnye khochitsa peet*/мне хочется пить
this *etat* **(m)**, *eta* **(f)**, *eta* **(n)**/этот, эта, это
those *tye*/те
throat *gorla*/горло
through *cheryiz*/через
ticket *beelyet*/билет
tickets *beelyetiy*/билеты
tie *galstook*/галстук
tight (dress) *tyesniy*/тесный
(shoes) *oozkee*/узкий
tights *kalgotkee*/колготки
time *vremya*/время
(first etc.) *raz*/раз
what's the time? *katoriy chas?*/который час?
timetable *raspeesaneeye*/расписание
tin *banka*/банка
tin-opener *kansyervniy nozh*/консервный нож
tired *oostal* **(m)**, *oostala* **(f)**, *oostalee* **(pl)**/устал, устала, устали
to *f*/в, *na*/на, *k*/к
(up to, until) *da*/до
tobacco *tabak*/табак
today *sivodnya*/сегодня
together *fmyestye*/вместе
toilet *twalyet*/туалет
toilet paper *twalyetnaya boomaga*/туалетная бумага
tomato *pameedor*/помидор
tomato juice *tamatniy sok*/томатный сок
tomorrow *zaftra*/завтра
tonight *sivodnya vyecheram*/сегодня вечером
too *sleeshkam*/слишком
too (as well) *takzhe*/также
tooth *zoop*/зуб
toothbrush *zoopnaya shchotka*/зубная щётка
toothpaste *zoopnaya pasta*/зубная паста

tourist *tooreest* (*ka*)/турист (ка)
towel *palatyentse*/ полотенце
tower ***bash**nya*/башня
town ***go**rat*/город
town centre *tsentr **go**rada*/ центр города
toy *ee**groosh**ka*/игрушка
traffic lights *svyeta**for***/ светофор
train ***poy**ezd*/поезд
traveller's cheque *da**rozh**niy chek*/дорожный чек
tree ***dyer**eva*/дерево
trip *pa**yezd**ka*/поездка
trousers ***bryoo**kee*/брюки
to try on *preemir**yat***/ примерять
T-shirt ***ma**ika*/майка
to turn *pavyer**noot***/ повернуть

U
umbrella ***zon**teek*/зонтик
uncle ***dya**dya*/дядя
under *pod*/под
underpants *kal**so**niy*/ калсоны
underground (subway) *mi**tro***/ метро
to understand *panee**mat***, *pan**yat***/понимать, понять
do you understand? *viy panee**ma**yetye?*/вы понимаете?
unfortunately *k sazha**lyen**iyoo*/ к сожалению
university *ooneevirseet**yet***/ университет
until *da*/до
upstairs *navir**khoo***/наверху
us *nas*/нас
to us *nam*/нам
USA *Sayedeen**yon**iye **Sht**atiy*/Соединённые Штаты

V
vacant *sva**bod**na*/свободно
valuable ***tsyen**niy*/ценный
veal *til**ya**teena*/телятина
vegetables ***o**vashchee*/овощи
vegetarian *vigitaree**an**ets* (**m**), *vigitaree**an**ka* (**f**)/ вегетарианец, вегетарианка
very ***o**chin*/очень
vest ***ma**ika*/майка
view *veed*/вид
village *sye**lo***/село
vinegar ***ook**soos*/уксус
visa ***vee**za*/виза
visit *pasyesh**chen**eeye*/ посещение
to visit *pasyesh**chat***, *pasye**teet***/посещать, посетить
voltage *napryaz**hen**eeye*/ напряжение

W
to wait for *zhdat*/ждать
wait! *padazh**deet**ye!*/ подождите!
waiter *afeetsee**ant***/ официант
waitress *afeetsee**ant**ka*/ официантка; ***dye**vooshka*/девушка
waiting room *zal azhee**da**neeya*/зал ожидания
to wake (someone) *boo**deet***/ будить
Wales *Oo**els***/Уэльс
walk *pra**gool**ka*/прогулка
to walk *ee**tee***, *paee**tee***/идти, пойти
wall *sty**ena***/стена
to want *khat**yet***/хотеть
I want *ya kha**choo***/я хочу
wardrobe *shkaf*/шкаф
warm ***tyop**liy*/тёплый
to wash (clothes) *pastee**rat***/ постирать
(self) ***miyt**sa*/мыться
(hair) ***viy**miyt*/вымыть
washbasin *oomiy**val**neek*/ умывальник
watch *cha**siy***/часы

water *va**da***/вода
we *miy*/мы
week *nid**yel**ya*/неделя
to weigh ***vye**seet*/весить
Welsh *oo**el**skee*/уэльский
west ***za**pat*/запад
wet ***mo**kriy*/мокрый
what *shto*/что; *ka**koy***/ какой
wheel *kalye**so***/колесо
when *kag**da***/когда
where *gdye*/где
  where from *atkoo**da***/ откуда
  where to *koo**da***/куда
which *ka**to**riy*/который
which? *ka**koy**?*/какой?
while *pa**ka***/пока
white ***bye**liy*/белый
who *kto*/кто
whole ***tsyel**iy*/целый
why *pache**moo***/почему
wide *shee**ro**kee*/широкий
wife *zhe**na***/жена
to win ***vi**yeegrat*/выиграть
wind ***vye**tir*/ветер
window *ak**no***/окно
wine *vee**no***/вино
winter *zee**ma***/зима
with *s*/с
without *byez*/без
woman ***zhen**shcheena*/ женщина
wood *lyes*/лес
wool *shairst*/шерсть
wonderful *vileeka**lyep**niy*/ великолепный
work *ra**bo**ta*/работа
to work *ra**bo**tat*/работать
  ... doesn't work *... ni ra**bo**tayet*/... не работает
to be worth ***sto**yeet*/стоить
to wrap *zav**yor**tiyvat*/ завёртывать
to write *pee**sat**, napee**sat***/ писать, написать
  write it down! *napee**sheet**ye*!/напишите!
writing paper *pach**to**vaya boo**ma**ga*/почтовая бумага
wrong *ni**pra**veelniy*/ неправильный

X
X-ray ***rint**gyen*/рентген

Y
year *god*/год
yellow ***zhol**tiy*/жёлтый
yes *da*/да
yesterday *fche**ra***/вчера
yoghurt *prastak**va**sha*/ простокваша
you *viy*/вы;
  (child) *tiy*/ты;
  (as object) *vas*/вас, *tib**ya***/ тебя
  to you *vam*/вам, *tib**ye***/ тебе
young *mala**doy***/молодой
your *vash* **(m)**, ***va**sha* **(f)**, ***va**she* **(n)**, ***va**shee* **(pl)**/ваш, ваша, ваше, ваши
  (child) *tvoy* **(m)**, *tva**ya*** **(f)**, *tva**yo*** **(n)**, *tvaee* **(pl)**/твой, твая, твоё, твои

Z
zoo *zoo**park***/зоопарк